The Practice of
TIBETAN
MEDITATION

The Practice of

TIBETAN
MEDITATION

EXERCISES, VISUALIZATIONS,
AND MANTRAS
FOR HEALTH AND WELL-BEING

DAGSAY TULKU RINPOCHE

Inner Traditions
Rochester, Vermont

Inner Traditions International
One Park Street
Rochester, Vermont 05767
www.InnerTraditions.com

First U.S. edition published by Inner Traditions International in 2002
Originally published in German under the title *Das Praxisbuch der Tibetischen Meditation*
by Lama Dagsay Tulku

LIBRARY OF CONGRESS CATALOGING-IN-PUBLICATION DATA
Tulku, Lama Dagsay
The Practice of Tibetan Meditation : exercises, visualizations, and
mantras for health and well-being / Lama Dagsay Tulku.
p. cm.
ISBN 0-89281-903-0
1. Meditation—Buddhism. 2. Buddhism—China—Tibet—Doctrines.
3. Healing—Religious aspects—Buddhism. I. Title.
BQ7805 .Z37 2002
294.3'4435—dc21
2001004814

Printed and bound in Canada

10   9   8   7   6   5   4   3   2   1

Text design and layout by Virginia L. Scott Bowman
This book was typeset in Garamond with Ellington and Gill Sans Condensed as the display typefaces.

Contents

Acknowledgments

IN WRITING THIS PRACTICE-ORIENTED BOOK on Tibetan meditation, it has been my deepest desire to open the gates to inner peace for people in many walks of life. I wish to express my gratitude to those who have helped me to realize the dream and to complete this book.

First, I want to thank my son-in-law Dr. Kalsang Shak who gave me the idea to write this book and encouraged me to see it through. My daughter Dechen also helped me with her untiring support. Her intelligence and ability to interpret the subject at hand with a great deal of sensitivity were put into action to translate complicated concepts into the English language. Without her help I would not have been able to develop the meditation and physical exercises. Special thanks go to my wife, Yishi-Tshedön, who has been supportive not only of this project but also in all areas of my life.

Even today I am very much in debt to my professor of philosophy Khensur Lobsang Thupten. He took me into his care during my years of study at the University of Sera in Lhasa. In addition, I wish to thank my many students who have guided me in understanding Western thought. I am also grateful to Inner Traditions International for publishing this book.

The deepest gratitude I owe to my teacher Monk Rigzin Dorje, who passed away a few years ago. He instructed me in the basics of Buddhist philosophy, and I was privileged to be under his guidance from age five to eighteen in the Chokri Monastery.

Preface

AMONG PEOPLE IN THE WEST, the need for inner peace has increased tremendously in recent years. As one of the first Tibetan Lamas to have settled in the West about four decades ago, I feel a great need to open the gate to Tibetan meditation, which comes from my experience as a monk in the spiritual world of a monastery and as a citizen of the world.

It is my innermost desire to pass on the valuable instructions for Tibetan meditation to everyone, regardless of creed or age, and to do so in a manner easily understood by everyone. Therefore, I wish to encourage people who are comfortable in their own beliefs to use Tibetan meditation as a means to strengthen their spirituality. I also recommend meditation to people who are not associated with any specific belief because they also can profit from it in many ways.

We are truly convinced that the sources of many of the adversities we face, including our own unhappiness, are external ones. Therefore, we frequently overlook the all-important inner perspective. Only after experiencing inner peace will we be able to radiate peace to the outside. In other words we then will be able to prominently contribute to a positive environment for ourselves and for the people around us. Thus, everyone has the potential to contribute to peace on earth. It is my deepest desire to see the greatest possible number of people choosing this path to peace.

With the help of this book on Tibetan meditation, I wish to provide practical instruction to all people in the world to achieve inner peace and serenity and lead them to the source of love and compassion. Only upon living in unity with this source and by taking from the source will we be able to radiate peace and contribute to positive surroundings.

Introduction

WHILE LIVING IN THE CHOKRI MONASTERY in Tehor in eastern Tibet, I was accustomed to being treated with utmost respect because of my status as a reincarnation of one of the principal Lamas. It was taken for granted that the honorable Dagsay was to be served at all times and that he would not deal with ordinary people. That was to soon change. Thousands of my fellow citizens and I were forced to flee Tibet in 1959. We were housed in bamboo barracks in a refugee camp provided by the Indian government. It could have been a great deal worse but, luckily, I was allowed to leave the camp after a few months when I received a scholarship at the University of Benares. When I graduated at the top of the class, I received an offer to teach at the University of Allahabad. There was no question about accepting this once-in-a-lifetime opportunity, and I invited all my friends to a farewell party. Exactly one day before I was to leave, I received a personal note from His Holiness the Fourteenth Dalai Lama. He asked me to go to Switzerland in the position of a spiritual teacher for Tibetan refugees. This posed a dilemma. Again, this situation taught me how things are always changing and that happiness and sorrow will take turns in the eternal rhythm of life. It was a great honor for me to have been chosen by His Holiness to fulfill this task, and I decided to follow his calling. When I arrived at the airport in Zurich in 1963, I had no clue what was in store for me in that new world.

I was on a bus together with other people from my country, all of us there to build a new existence. We were all in the same predicament. Everyone soon got used to the new circumstances, and spiritual values were pushed temporarily aside by material needs, which, for the time being, made my role as spiritual leader superfluous. Thus, I had to look for another job. I found an apprenticeship in construction drafting, I met my wife, and we planned our future together.

Despite the fact that life with our three children was happy and content, I was frequently haunted by my escape from Tibet. Those events had left traces of deepest fear, despair, and helplessness that came to life in my nightmares. A daily practice of meditation and proper mental training enabled me, however, to transform those feelings of hate and aggression that were causing me harm into sentiments of compassion and love.

My inner peace returned—it happened in just the same manner as at the Chokri Monastery long ago. Colleagues at my work were frequently amazed at my inner calm and serenity even during intense moments when everyone else was on edge. Without being consciously aware of the situation, I constantly benefited from the great treasure of Tibetan meditation, which created a positive environment and a basis for peaceful coexistence.

The two worlds I had experienced in my life were very different from each other: the eastern Tibetan world, dominated by the desire to obtain spiritual values, and the Western world, where material values are in the foreground. Yet both worlds have one thing in common: Tibetan meditation applies itself well to both ways of life. As the years passed, my experiences of monastery life in the East were augmented by those of everyday life in the West, and I became more and more convinced that the use of meditation could be completely independent of religion.

After twenty-two years, relations with China improved and I was able to contact my relatives at home. Soon there followed letters from my monastery.

I was asked to return home and resume my spiritual position as a Lama. Upon my arrival thousands of people were waiting for my blessings and initiations. This trip was to change my future life in Switzerland. My family and our relatives started to support the reconstruction of the monastery and, in addition, we began to work on the project of an adjacent clinic, which was to include a training center for Tibetan meditation. (More information is provided in the "Seminars and Projects" section at the end of the book.)

My experiences as a Lama in the West have taught me that many meditations can be carried out not only on a spiritual level but also in secular fashion. When I was a monk inside the monastery, it was unimaginable for me to meditate for other than spiritual reasons. While living in the West, where many people are members of a different creed, or have no religion at all, I became aware that possibly all people could make use of many of the Buddhist teachings.

To pass this knowledge on to as many people as possible, I have arranged it in such a way to make sense to everybody, whether they are Buddhist, non-Buddhist, a beginner, or an advanced student. These exercises are particularly helpful to people who suffer from the effects of today's fast-paced life and who are under physical and psychological pressure. These meditations—precious gems from the treasures of the higher Buddhist school of mind training—are helpful in all kinds of circumstances. Whether you are feeling low because of a failure or a problem at work, because something is worrying you, or because you have an illness, these exercises will take an active part in pulling you up; when you are feeling great because you are in perfect health and have been successful and lucky, the exercises will keep you from becoming arrogant and losing your grip.

ONE

What Is Meditation?

THE TIBETAN WORD FOR MEDITATION IS *GOM*. Literally translated it means "to become familiar with an object." This object is an item you get to know very well by concentrating your thinking on it. The item is called the "object of meditation." The object may be a flower, a candle, a picture, a sculpture, or the mind itself. Because the type of object will directly influence your mind, it is important to choose well. When you pick an object that triggers positive thoughts in your mind, you will experience a positive change, and your state of mind will become peaceful and at ease. If you choose an item that gives you negative feelings, your mind will be altered unfavorably, and you will be uncomfortable. In the case that your item has neutral value, your mind, in return, will remain unchanged.

Because we meditate in order to achieve something positive, it is obvious that one ought to choose a positive object for meditation. In traditional Tibetan meditation, objects are chosen that are fundamentally of a character that promotes healing.

By thinking deeply about the object at hand, we want to achieve a positive influence on our mind. Tibetan meditation provides us with a number of different techniques, which are carried out on two levels: meditation through *concentration* and through *analysis*. When we practice concentration meditation, we attach our mind to an object of meditation and are able to stay with it, allowing no distractions. This in turn provides the basis for analytical meditation, which, among other things, attempts to explore the true nature of an object of meditation in order to discover the final and true nature of phenomena. This kind of recognition is a prerequisite in achieving Buddhahood, the complete enlightenment and the final goal of meditation in Tibetan Buddhism.

Buddhists believe that all our actions are dependent on our state of mind; an unhealthy outlook will cause suffering, and therefore the mind itself is the principal object of meditation. I like to talk about the "taming" of the mind. A mind that is not well controlled is liable to cause a great deal of harm to itself and others, while a peaceful mind creates a comfortable atmosphere for itself and everyone around. Therefore meditation also serves to harmonize body and mind, as well as creates a balanced state of inner and outer peace.

Why do we meditate?

All living creatures—humans and all animals down to the smallest insect—have one thing in common: they all long for happiness and well-being. Nobody wants to suffer.

You may have spent some time in your life watching the comings and goings of a busy ant colony. The ants busily race from one place to another. In their own way, they are looking for some kind of satisfaction, some sort of well-being.

I look upon humans in a similar fashion. During our relatively short life span of no more than eighty to a hundred years, we follow a steady daily routine: We work, eat, drink, and sleep, and are constantly striving to attain happiness and well-being. Then why is it that we are unable to be happy and content at all times?

In addition to the four basic reasons for suffering—birth, old age, illness, and death—there are always other forms of suffering that cast shadow on our lives. Countless problems originate from a faulty internal outlook and contribute to the fact that happiness never lasts for too long. Soured relations between people, stress at work, financial worries, problems in raising one's children, and other factors may all cause unhappiness.

Because we are lazy, we tend to look for the causes of distress in external circumstances. We are often able to quickly find a culprit in the wrongdoing of others. In the long run, though, this strategy turns out to be very tiring, because it leads to the fact that the problems never change. It does not help to keep blaming others because the only result is a substitution of causes, while all along the true reason for suffering can only be found by looking to your inner self.

Tibetan doctors and Lamas are convinced that only by cutting the root cause can illness be healed. Treating the symptoms will cause no more than a temporary cure. If you look inside, on the other hand, you will discover the reasons for your suffering are caused by the disposition of your mind. According to Tibetan Buddhism, all suffering is self-inflicted. The other side of the coin, however, points to the fact that we ourselves are the makers of our happiness.

TWO

Strategies for Working with This Book

THERE ARE THREE LEVELS OF DIFFICULTY to the exercises provided throughout this book:

Easy ❖
These exercises require no experience in meditation or visualization. They are, however, still interesting for people with advanced knowledge.

Medium ❖ ❖
You can do the exercises in this category after you have had some experience in meditation and visualization. Beginners who are ready for a next step can also try these exercises.

Difficult ❖ ❖ ❖
To carry out these exercises, you should already be able to visualize well (i.e., able to see certain shapes and colors at the same time).

To facilitate the quick identification of appropriate exercises for your specific practice, look for what you need in the overview tables in the Appendix. (You should, however, read the entire book.)

Using Visualization

Each exercise in this book will suggest appropriate images to visualize during that particular practice. If you have never used visualization before, I recommend that you take an object that resembles the suggested image and place it in front of you at eye level. Now take a good look and memorize all details of the object before you start with the meditation itself. This process will assist you with more precise and effective visualization during the exercise.

Mantras and Mudras

There are certain hand movements, *mudras,* and healing syllables, *mantras,* associated with many of the exercises. Mudras and mantras intensify the effect of each specific exercise. If you do not feel at ease with the exercise, you can first do it without the use of the mudras and mantras, and then add them later.

Mudras are certain gestures, movements, or body positions. The finger mudras are the most commonly known mudras. Here, the fingers are held in a prescribed position in order to cause a physical, mental, or spiritual effect.

Mantras are syllables that are very powerful, and they are known to have healing properties. The literal translation for mantra is "guarding the mind from negative influence." The origin of these ancient healing syllables goes back to the Vedic civilization, more than 4,000 years ago. A mantra is generally an act of respectfully addressing a designated deity for the purpose of requesting his or her cleansing nectar to purify one's transgressions, such as hate, greed, and ignorance. In addition, one uses the mantra to ask for the protection of these same deities.

Mantras have a central role in Buddha's teachings; therefore, the mantras that were passed on through Buddha are believed to have particular healing power. One recites the syllables in their original form while performing a meditation. Some of the longer mantras have an abbreviated version that is equal in strength and effect to the shorter versions. It makes for a particularly beautiful encounter to sing the mantras and be engulfed in their vibrations. It is also very relaxing to simply listen to the steady repetition of the sound of the syllables, allowing yourself to sink into your deepest inner states, even when you are not engaged in a particular exercise.

You may do any or all of the following: Say the mantras to yourself in a low voice, sing them loudly, recite them mentally, or simply listen to them. The effect of the mantras will be enhanced when you recite them in a steady, repetitive sequence of sounds.

Using the accompanying CD

This book comes with a CD containing nineteen recorded mantras that correspond to and enhance specific meditations. Throughout the text, each mantra is referenced by name and CD track number within the appropriate exercises. Before performing a meditation, it is advisable to listen to the recorded mantra for pronunciation assistance. If you are not familiar with the meditation, you may decide to listen to the CD throughout the exercise rather than recite the mantra yourself. As your comfort builds, you may choose to recite the mantra either with the CD or independently. You should not, however, begin reciting a mantra during a meditation until you are accustomed to the visualization process, or you will lose your focus.

How the book is organized

In Part One you will learn about the preliminary practices. I list nine points to assist you in harmonizing body and mind and to prepare them for the meditation session in the best possible manner. At the times when you are unable to observe and follow all nine steps, you still should complete the part on renewing your motivation before you proceed with the meditation.

Part Two of the book deals with meditations, such as the nectar purification, ray-of-light purification, or the concentration of healing power, performed for the purpose of easing various forms of suffering. These exercises have a noticeably comforting and energizing effect on your mind and body and have a spontaneously direct way of guiding you back to your center, where you will be able to find peace. This kind of serenity is particularly needed to face the ups and downs of everyday life in our hectic times. In addition, you will also learn to get in touch with the source for loving-kindness and compassion that is pres-ent in all of us.

I have dedicated one of the chapters to the subject of helping people who are dying. You will find many valuable guidelines, which are meant to assist the dying person in the process of transforming an apparently hopeless situa-tion into a state of meaningfulness. Here, I also wish to address the relatives and other people who are close to the dying person and help them with use-ful advice and specific instructions for the meditation.

Part Three describes the exercises that teach you how to overcome the cause of your suffering. Not only will you learn about how to ease your suffering but also about how to avoid the source of suffering in the future. There are, for example, valuable instructions on concentration and analytical meditation, such as the meditation on patience and tolerance, the meditation on imper-manence, and the meditation on emptiness. These instructions offer a logical and analytical angle to go to the source of our suffering and to help us avoid suffering in the future.

Also in Part Three are the seven Khum-Lhö massages for relaxation, as well as seven Lü-Gom exercises to relax and loosen up your body. These may be used at any time, whenever they are needed.

> A practicing Buddhist sees his or her daily routine in two phases: the time for sessions and the time in between sessions. During the time for sessions, the Buddhist meditates; the rest of the time is the time in between sessions. It is the Buddhist's task to train his or her mind according to the methods of higher Buddhist mental practices and, subsequently, to integrate the things that have been learned during the time in between sessions.

All three parts contain exercises that cater to beginners and advanced stu-dents of meditation. It is most important for you to set in practice what you have learned from your meditations. Do not worry, everyday life will provide you with everlasting opportunities for practice to do so. Concentration, for example, refers not only to the kind of meditation itself but also to an array of daily routines. You observe how, when, and under what circumstances your concentration will trail off while you are working, while you are talking to somebody, or even while you are watching television. With whom do you lack patience or compassion—with yourself, a partner, family members, friends, or foes? What about your ability to be tolerant toward those who think or act differently, or look different than you? Be alert and you will find countless opportunities to implement what you have learned during meditation. However, allow yourself some breaks during which you can relax and act like a normal person.

When taking up meditation, one follows a learning process similar to that of other subjects. In challenging yourself, it is important to neither overdo it nor ask too little of yourself, in order to avoid frustration or boredom. Do not fall prey to unrealistic ambitions; it is very important to find the correct measure, which is equivalent, in principle, to the dosage of medical drugs. Take ample time to experience and live through the various steps. Whenever you get tired, relax by doing the massages or exercises. Beginners in particular are strongly advised to become well acquainted with the first part of this book, and even those who are advanced will find many details and helpful hints with which they are not yet familiar.

> He who merely sits down to meditate and never strives to implement that which he has learned in his everyday life has failed to grasp the essence of Tibetan meditation.

The book ends with the closing remarks, my seven wish-fulfilling jewels, and the summary table, "Specific Applications in Tibetan Meditation" in the Appendix. In the Annotated Bibliography are listed complementary books to further introduce and expand one's knowledge in Tibetan meditation, as well as books that focus on a particular subject of meditation. The index allows you to search for specific terms throughout the book. If you are interested in intensifying your meditation practices, you will find information on my seminars on page 156.

PART ONE

Preliminary Practices

IT HAS BEEN SAID ABOUT ONE of the famous Lamas, who was quite accomplished in Tibetan meditation, that he was able to complete a meditation on a certain subject in the time it took to mount his horse. This shows that it may be possible for a meditation to take place in the short time between the moment of setting one's foot into the stirrup and sitting down on the horse, without going through the motions of preliminary practices.

This example further illustrates that meditation is not tied to a certain location or time. There are, however, only a few people who are able to do this, and therefore I recommend that you follow nine steps before you start the meditation itself. Soon you will find out for yourself that a trained mind will require less and less time to go through an exercise. A fundamental idea in meditation is the following:

> You will achieve your goal with patience
> and perseverance.

Preparing for Meditation

Where to meditate

If you desire to implement meditation firmly in your everyday life, you need to find a quiet spot in your house or apartment. It would be helpful to be able to use the same place every time you meditate in order for your mind and body to quickly adapt to the meditative setting. There is no need for this place to be large or for it to be arranged in an elaborate manner. Choose a spot that makes you feel good and comfortable. But you are also free to choose a place to meditate other than the location you picked in your house; that is the one of the beauties of meditation. It is not necessary to take a sitting position with your legs crossed or the lotus position. You can meditate at any place in any position. You may be walking, riding a train or a subway, or sitting on a bench. My students always chuckle when I advise them not to meditate while driving a car or at work.

Cushion and clothing for meditation

If you plan to sit down for a long period of time, you will need a good foundation to sit on, such as a soft blanket or a cushion. This will support your efforts to keep your spine straight while also easing the pressure on your thighs. The cushion should be neither too hard nor too soft. The cushions that are most suitable for beginners are of a round, moonlike shape. I have learned that people in the West may find it difficult to sit down on the ground and take up a lotus position. Therefore, I would encourage you to take up a customary position and sit on a chair. Wear loose-fitting clothes, preferably made from natural fibers, so as not to feel uncomfortable and distracted by tightness during the meditation.

Time of meditation

Following monastery tradition and from my personal experience, meditation is undoubtedly most effective at dawn, because the mind's perception is at its peak during this time of the day. Your sleep at night has left it rested, clear, and open to suggestion; most important, it has not yet been worried by all kinds of troubling thoughts. Should you belong to the group of people unable to give up the beauty of morning slumber, despite all your resolve and earnest effort, you could practice meditation in the evening.

During the day it is also possible to conduct a meditation in the form of a short contemplation while you are carrying out simple tasks or while you are walking. This may have a reviving and invigorating effect. For example, when you go for a walk, take a break, sit down under a tree, and take in the landscape and the beauty of nature. At a later point, when you have gained experience with meditation, you can also become aware of the tree's impermanence (see the exercise beginning on page 131).

Preparing the body

Apart from those times when you are doing a short contemplation that takes place spontaneously and needs no preparation, you should get your body ready before entering a meditation.

Avoid drinking beverages that stimulate you, such as black tea, coffee, or alcohol. Instead, you could enjoy a warming and calming herbal tea. Have a little something to eat to avoid feelings of hunger; your stomach should be neither stuffed nor empty. With your bladder and bowels relieved, you will be able to improve your concentration on the meditation. Because breathing techniques are a part of the meditation, you also should blow your nose well and get rid of mucus in your upper lungs.

Preparing the mind

To motivate yourself, decide ahead of time on the duration of your meditation. Do not take too much upon yourself; otherwise, you may run the risk of quickly losing joy and enthusiasm in meditation. Experienced monks like to compare meditation to a meal: When you get ready to prepare a meal for yourself, you take into consideration the size of your appetite. If your appetite is great, your preparations take more time. You will have to buy more at the store, then cook the appropriate amount, and finally, enjoy your meal. If you are a little hungry, you will buy less, prepare a little, and enjoy it as well. If you prepare too little at the times when you are very hungry and you are not satisfied, it will cause you to be unhappy. Neither will you be content if you are only a little hungry but you eat too much.

It is important to estimate your need for meditation before you get started in order to avoid such feelings of dissatisfaction.

FOUR

Seven Elements of Correct Posture

ACCORDING TO TIBETAN TRADITION, people meditate while sitting. You can adapt the body posture accordingly, however, depending on the type of meditation you are currently practicing—when doing a short contemplation, for example. Therefore, it is possible to meditate while lying down in case of illness or other physical challenges. But, in general, you should avoid the lying-down position simply because it is more comfortable, because part of teaching the mind involves overcoming laziness. Physical discipline will enhance mental discipline and improve your ability to concentrate. Without discipline, your mind is apt to wander, which is a great hindrance to meditation.

Buddhists strive for correct posture and sitting position because Buddha himself, 2,500 years ago, became enlightened as the Buddha while sitting in this position.

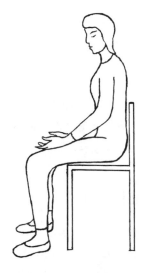

Correct Posture Sitting on Floor   Correct Posture Sitting on Chair

Legs

The customary position of the legs is the lotus position. You sit on the floor with your legs crossed while your ankles rest on your thighs. Your right leg is folded on top of your left leg. It takes a lot of patience to master this position in the beginning. Therefore, take ample time and do not push yourself.

Lotus Position   Half-lotus Position

You also have the option to sit in the half-lotus position. Here, you simply tuck in your left ankle and leave the right leg loosely bent in front.

Sit down on a cushion to elevate your pelvis above your legs. This decreases the pressure on the legs.

If this is still too strenuous, you may sit on a chair. Make sure that the chair's backrest is a straight one. Then sit on the front part of the seat, without resting your back. Allow your legs to rest comfortably over the edge of the chair, with the soles of your feet touching the ground.

Hands and arms

Tibetan tradition recommends resting both hands on your lap just an inch below your navel. The right hand rests in the left one with both thumbs pushing lightly against each other.

Some forms of Tibetan meditation suggest resting your hands on your knees with the palms facing up.

Try out both positions to determine the one that best suits you.

Avoid pressing your arms into your body; instead, let them hang about a fist's width from your body.

Hands Resting on the Knees

Traditional Tibetan Hand Position

Back

Try to keep your back as straight as possible without straining. Your spine should be as straight as possible for the energy to flow freely. Free-flowing energy has a positive effect on meditation, for both mind and body.

Mouth

Your mouth should be relaxed and in a natural position, with the tip of your tongue lightly touching your palate. This will keep your mouth moist but at the same time inhibit the flow of saliva down your chin during an intense meditation that may last for a long time.

Eyes

Keep your eyes slightly open, looking down along your nose to the ground. If you find it easier to concentrate by closing your eyes, do so in the beginning. Make sure you do not fall asleep or get lost in dreams.

Head

Your head should be bent forward slightly, with your chin gently tucked in.

Shoulders

Consciously relax your shoulders and let them hang loosely.

FIVE

Observing Your State of Mind

THIS PARTICULAR PREPARATION FOR MEDITATION is meant to familiarize you with the normal daily flow of your thoughts and consciously observe them being at incessant play.

Take up your preferred position of meditation and check the seven elements of posture. At this point let your imagination run free for about three minutes and calmly observe—not unlike a shepherd keeping a watchful eye on his sheep—all the places your busy mind is going.

During the next step try to keep your mind in check as much as possible for another three minutes—comparable to the shepherd who has to gather his sheep at night in order to take them to the stable.

While you are trying to gather your thoughts, remain calm and collected. Pay close attention to the manner in which you are achieving this task. Don't worry if you are not able to do this right away. To my students, I sometimes recommend writing down the thoughts that come up during these three minutes.

Most of the time this presents a rather interesting picture of their world of thoughts. (I myself am frequently impressed by the scope of the journeys my mind is taking, how it reaches into the past and the future, and how hard at work it is within this short period of time.)

You can put together a worksheet for this exercise as suggested on the following pages; this will facilitate your routine and, at the same time, give you an overview of your mind's journeys.

Renew your motivation

A first step to successful meditation is motivation. Motivation is the most important preliminary element to possess before embarking on any action. What is the meaning of motivation?

Motivation is a very strong determination to achieve a goal. For example, an athlete is full of motivation to win the race or at least do his or her best. If one lacked strong willpower of this sort, one's performance would be meager. To follow this example, we need to muster the right kind of motivation every time we meditate. Therefore, it is of great importance for anyone who wishes to meditate to muster awareness before the meditation and resolve to follow the exercises at hand with enthusiasm, without allowing any distraction.

When you are aware of your goal—the positive effect of the meditation in the form of physical, mental, and spiritual relaxation—it will become much easier for you to completely finish the meditation. Because mind and body have very strong ties to each other, the importance of motivation can be stated as follows: The stronger your determination, the more profound the effect of the meditation.

It is important to renew your motivation immediately before you start each meditation, and to do so with great conviction. In that instant you wholeheartedly resolve to pass the time you have set aside for meditation with the greatest intensity and without allowing your thoughts to wander. The effect of your meditation thus will have been improved manifold. This is the reason the following preliminary actions, as well as the main meditation, are initiated by consciously renewing motivation.

WORKSHEET 1

Relaxed Contemplation of One's Thoughts

Date and Time of Meditation:

Where does my mind wander?

1 _____

2 _____

3 _____

4 _____

5 _____

6 _____

7 _____

8 _____

9 _____

10 _____

11 _____

12 _____

WORKSHEET 2

Observing Thoughts, Collecting Them with Care, and Determining the Duration of Time One Is Able to Hold On to a Thought

Date and Time of Meditation:

	Where do my thoughts wander?	Am I able to gather my thoughts?	How long am I able to hold on to a thought?
1			
2			
3			
4			
5			
6			
7			
8			
9			
10			
11			
12			

Breathing Technique for the Ninefold Purification of Energy

A PEACEFUL AND RELAXED MIND IS a prerequisite to meaningful meditation. Breathing techniques as they are taught in Tibetan tradition are millennia-old methods with great contemporary appeal because they harmonize body and soul quickly and effectively. Breathing brings about life! Despite the fact that we take breathing for granted, it still has the most important function in our body: It keeps us alive. When you pinch your nose and close your mouth for a moment, you soon discover how dependent you are on breathing. The manner in which you breathe is, further, a mirror of your psychological state of mind: When you are nervous or excited, you breathe hastily, and when you are peaceful and balanced inside you breathe calmly. Therefore, you are able to control your breathing to calm down, to influence your psychological state when it becomes necessary.

The breathing technique for the ninefold purification of energy assists in bringing about the needed peace and quiet of the mind.

Both hands are resting in your lap (step one).

Step One

Slowly bring your left hand up to your nose while turning it palm out. Now press on your left nostril using your ring finger and start breathing slowly through your right nostril. Consciously hold your breath for a short time (step two).

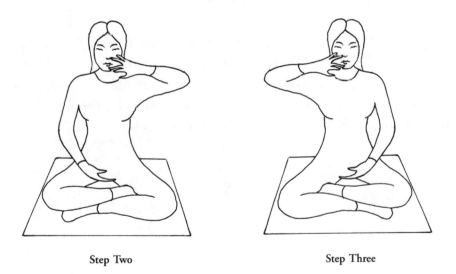

Step Two   Step Three

While you are holding your breath, lower your left hand and rest it in your lap, then slowly raise the right one, again turning out your palm and bringing it up to your nose. Take your right ring finger and use it to close your right nostril, then expel your breath slowly and with purpose through the left nostril (step three).

Repeat this exercise three times.

Now slowly bring your right hand up to your nose while turning it palm out. Press on your right nostril using your ring finger and start breathing slowly through your left nostril. Consciously then hold your breath for a short time (step four).

Step Four

While you are holding your breath, lower your right hand and rest it in your lap, then slowly raise the left one, again turning out your palm and bringing it up to your nose. Now take your left ring finger and use it to close your left nostril, then expel your breath slowly and with purpose through the right nostril (step five). Repeat this exercise three times as well.

Step Five

Finally, take three even breaths though both nostrils; hold your breath consciously and then expel it slowly and with purpose, using both nostrils. Your hands should be resting on your thighs (step six).

Step Six

Once you have become accustomed to this sequence, use all your imagination possible while breathing in and out, as well as when you are holding your breath.

- While you breathe *in,* imagine you are taking in a great amount of purifying energy.
- While you *hold your breath,* imagine that these forces are thoroughly purifying your mind as well as your body.
- While you breathe *out,* imagine how every conflict- and transgression-related element of your body or your mind is being expelled with your slow and determined breath.

Important considerations

Avoid taking quick breaths; instead, breathe gently and intently. While you are holding your breath, you should always be listening to your inner voice. Breathe out when you feel that you want to do so and let air return when you want to breathe in. Do not put any unnecessary pressure upon yourself. Adapt your breathing to the rhythm that suits you. While you are closing your nostril, remember to lift your elbow up slightly, which allows the chest to open and improves your breathing. Pay attention to staying with the exercise, not allowing your thoughts to drift off. To make this possible, say to yourself the following phrases with every breath you take.

- Slowly and deeply I breathe *in.*
- Gently my breath I *hold.*
- Slowly and with purpose I breathe *out.*

Everyone has a different technique of breathing deeply; therefore, it is important to listen to one's inner voice and adjust this exercise in breathing to one's needs. Some people will experience nausea or dizziness when their breathing in is too long or too short, as well as when they exhale too slowly or too rapidly. Because of that, take an occasional normal breath while you are doing the exercise.

SEVEN

Breathing Exercise for Harmonizing Body and Soul

❖

THIS EXERCISE SERVES THE SAME PURPOSE OF harmonizing body and soul and is used at times when the mind has not been neutralized despite the ninefold purification of energy. However, this does not mean that you may only use this exercise at times when you have been unsuccessful with the ninefold purification of energy. On the contrary, this exercise is very popular among my students and holds an important place among the preparations for meditation.

In general, our minds are constantly subject to various distractions. This is the reason we use a goal-oriented method to try and keep the mind from any kind of distraction, and to keep it neutral. Breathing, here, is the foremost tool to keep the mind from wandering. Furthermore, this exercise has a positive influence on the physical and psychological aspects of human life and is important in supporting the meditation.

As in all exercises, start by checking your posture. Now breathe in slowly and gently through your nose, hold your breath for a short time, and breathe out slowly and gently again.

31

Inhaling, holding your breath briefly, and exhaling are counted as one unit. Following Tibetan custom this exercise is repeated at least seven times. Depending on your need, you may repeat it any uneven number of times until your mind has settled down noticeably.

When you do this exercise, remember to keep concentrating on your breathing in and out. Therefore, accompany your breathing mentally as shown in the following examples:

- When you *inhale,* think, "I am breathing in."
- When you *hold* your breath, think, "I am holding my breath."
- When you *exhale,* think, "I am breathing out."

Your mind is thus constant company to your breathing, which means that you are traveling by means of your mind into your body. A Tibetan saying expresses the action vividly: "The mind is riding on breathing's back."

Allow your mind to journey to your innermost place. Consciously experience your breath traveling in through both nostrils, the windpipe, and then into your lungs. See in your mind's eye how your lungs fill with life-giving oxygen, how it slightly stretches your chest, and how your lungs are serviced with this precious energy, which nourishes every small cell in your body through this unique force of our universe.

While you are *holding your breath,* imagine with all your heart how equilibrium is being created in every cell of your body.

While you are *exhaling,* occupy yourself in watching your breath leaving the body the same way it came in. Notice that it is expelled slowly but purposefully and how every little bit is being sent out of your body. With every new breath, you will feel the harmonization of body and mind. But do not breathe out too quickly in order to avoid becoming short of breath.

At the beginning, a stabilization of body and mind may be dependent on your state of mind before you start a meditating session. Therefore, you should avoid meditation when you experience an outbreak of extreme emotions, whether positive or negative. Let a little time pass to settle your emotions before you embark on a meditation. If you practice meditation regularly, you will, in time, develop the ability to conduct the exercise flawlessly, despite obstacles of that kind.

When you are unable to get rid of those thoughts that you wish to expel, don't let that discourage you. Just take a little break in order to avoid anger and disappointment, and then start from the beginning.

At first your meditations ought to be of short duration. Only gradually you will want to spend more time. Remember the analogy with the meal: It is important to strike the right balance. Interruptions, therefore, can be very helpful in increasing your motivation to meditate. The time it takes to prepare for the meditation depends on you. In general, it takes about twenty-one breaths before you get that positive sensation of being relaxed and of your body and mind being in harmony.

Remain loose, relaxed, and unperturbed during this preparation for the meditation. That is how you avoid overexerting yourself and suffering side effects, such as being dazed, shivering, or sensing a shortness of breath.

Breathe very naturally and in a relaxed manner. It is up to you how much time you spend inhaling and exhaling and how you adapt the rhythm of this exercise to the breathing you are used to.

PART TWO

Meditations for Relieving
Suffering and for Bringing
About Happiness and
Contentment

ACCORDING TO BUDDHIST VIEW, every living being on earth is subject to four major forms of suffering: birth, illness, old age, and death. In addition, there exist countless forms of suffering that we are exposed to on a daily basis. Situations that make us suffer, for instance, are those times when we desire something but we cannot have it, or when an event takes a different course than we would have liked. It makes us unhappy when we have to separate from loved ones, when we lose respect, or when friends turn into foes, and we suffer when uncontrollable natural disasters occur.

Nobody is able to avoid suffering; however, people have developed various techniques to circumvent it. Many of us have succeeded in mastering denial and in playing down suffering. Frequently, this causes suffering to pop up in an altered form, such as in aggression, hate, or anger. Tibetan meditation instructs us to deal with suffering in a different way. It teaches us to ease suffering and gives us ideas on how to recognize the sources of suffering. In this part of the book, you will get well acquainted with the methods that will help you to ease suffering and even conquer it.

Why can meditation help to ease suffering?

Not long ago, people in the West used to doubt the interconnection of body and mind, but today it is generally accepted that one's state of mind has a great impact on one's physical well-being. Even psychologists and physicians are now convinced that there is a definite interconnection of the mind and the body. In Tibetan thinking, this idea has always been rooted firmly.

Just observe your body's behavior when you have an emotional reaction. The direct connection is immediately obvious: When you are overcome with anger, the blood rises to your head and you get very hot. Your face turns red, your eyes flash, and you clench your teeth. When you are sad, you can observe other bodily changes: Your chest tightens and your tear ducts produce tears.

People who, for instance, constantly have to bear stress and annoyances at home or at work will tense up and become inwardly nervous. If the situation persists and they are unable to relax mentally, their bodies will suffer as well, and they become prone to illnesses, such as ulcers or heart problems.

Every day you can observe and experience how much you depend on your state of mind. At the times when your mind is calm, relaxed, and content, your day will go well, and you won't get upset over the little things that go wrong. If, on the other hand, your mind is tense, nervous, and discontent, your day will be miserable, and the smallest problem will become big and insurmountable.

The methods of meditation in Tibetan Buddhism are built on this principle of interconnectedness of body and mind. Through these methods that I will introduce in this book, you will learn about the subtle and complicated mechanisms in the interaction of body, mind, and soul. These methods are part of the precious treasures of Tibetan meditation, and I present those that, from my experience, are particularly effective.

The meaning of visualization

A prerequisite for meditating, and for Tibetan meditations in particular, is the ability to visualize. Each and every one of us makes use of this ability whether or not we are conscious of it.

Visualization simply means using your memory to bring things that you have seen into the forefront of your thoughts or to imagine those things that you have never seen before. During the time when we think of images of any kind, such as our childhood or plans we have made for the future, certain emotions will be aroused simultaneously.

When we are doing the visual meditation, we visualize an image to invoke a certain state of mind that will directly affect our physical and mental concentration. That state of mind, in return, has an impact on your physical and spiritual well-being. Thus, it is not surprising that through visualization—when done correctly—it is possible to bring about physical and mental relaxation and start a process of healing, even in cases of serious illness. There are an increasing number of medical and psychological studies that confirm these interrelations.

Everybody subconsciously uses visualization. The question is how to make the best use of this ability. Deep visualization has always had a central position in Tibetan meditation and is recognized as the driving force in meditation. Ancient Tibetan writings contain practical instructions on how we can train ourselves to use this ability and implement it consciously.

The most important principle here is to apply your ability for visualization correctly. A correct application means that you visualize only those kinds of ideas, items, or subjects that have positive properties. Should you carelessly choose something that triggers negative emotions, then your visualization would automatically magnify the negative emotions, and you would become restless, nervous, or aggressive. By choosing a neutral subject or object for visualization, one that triggers neither bad nor good emotions, you would emphasize neutral emotions. A neutral emotion is not equivalent to a feeling of indifference, but rather is a feeling of peace of mind, free of any attachments or dislikes.

Because it is your desire to make the best use of the visualization, you will strive to have a positive, beautiful experience.

To achieve this, choosing a positive subject is necessary.

During the many years in my position as a Tibetan Lama in the West, I have discovered that the following meditations are the most beneficial, because they help all people, regardless of creed, achieve an invigorating and relaxing effect. In my instructions for the meditations, I have placed the main emphasis on carrying out an intensive technique of visualization to achieve that desired effect.

In Tibetan meditation, visual meditations are accepted as a practical and effective means to ease daily suffering. Visual meditation brings about happiness, contentedness, inner peace, and peace of mind. The following meditations will familiarize you with this method.

EIGHT

The Nectar Purification

NECTAR PURIFICATION IS A MOST POWERFUL meditation; it cleanses all negative energies originating in body or mind with nectar as the healing essence. When coupled with strong forces of visualization, this meditation will enable you to open up to your deepest inner layers and to rid yourself of all your negative emotions.

The nectar purification can be practiced on three levels: the Buddhist level, the level of people with different faiths, and the level of people who do not believe in a deity. The effect of the nectar purification is the same on all three levels. The differences are found in the choice for and in the meaning of the meditation object. Among Buddhists, the object of meditation for this purification exercise is the deity Vajra Sattva, who was specifically chosen for this purpose. People who are of a different faith will pick a holy being they are familiar with and that applies to the subject at hand. Christians, for instance, could put up a picture of Jesus or the Mother Mary. The picture or the figurine of that certain deity would need to be set up at eye level in order for the visualization to take place correctly. However, an atheist might imagine the object of meditation in the form of a powerful, positive, and warm body of light.

There are three forms of nectar purification known to Tibetan meditation. If you wish, you can combine each meditation with a certain mudra or mantra, or a combination of the two. These will intensify the experience of the meditation.

Overview

After you complete the customary preparations for the meditation, you are ready to begin with one of the three forms of nectar purification. Before starting the purification, you need to stabilize the object of meditation by using precise concentration—meaning that you attempt to visualize the object in as exact detail as possible and hold on to that image.

Once you have achieved this stabilization, you imagine your body being an empty vessel, as indicated in the instructions that follow. Then you compose yourself and focus your entire concentration on the object of meditation. This is the moment that will consciously fill you with great confidence in the healing and purifying power of the meditation object. You then conduct the exercise that you choose from one of the following three forms.

VAJRA SATTVA MANTRA (CD TRACK 1)

Particularly when practicing the nectar purification exercises, it makes sense to recite a healing mantra, such as the Vajra Sattva mantra below. It is also very relaxing just to listen to the words, which are recited on the accompanying CD, track 1.

> *Om vajra sattva hum,*
> *om vajra sattva,*
> *mama vyadhi,*
> *vibend adi sarva,*
> *nishedak perbava,*
> *shantim kuru svaha.*

FINISHING THE NECTAR PURIFICATION EXERCISES

Each of the three forms of nectar purification is ended by your imagining that white nectar is being poured all over you. Depending on the instructions, imagine the vessel of your body to be open on the top or on the bottom. The vessel fills with pure, healing nectar, and you let it all soak in.

IMPORTANT CONSIDERATIONS

If you do not yet know the nectar purification exercises, I recommend doing them in the beginning without the use of the mudras and mantras. When you have become quite familiar with the visualization of the nectar purification, you can add the mudras and/or mantras in order to intensify the sessions.

You can also play and recite the mantras on the CD, disregarding my instructions about the mudras and the breathing, simply breathing naturally.

The nature of the cleansing nectar may be beautifully warming or cool and refreshing. Depending on your mental or physical state, you can determine the properties of the nectar for yourself. For example, if you suffer from a fever, you can imagine the nectar to be cool and refreshing.

A prerequisite for all three kinds of purification is that you perform the exercises with absolute confidence and willpower. The nectar purification will not be effective unless you have total conviction and your concentration is strong and unwavering.

> There are three essential points to observe in order to obtain the best possible effect in nectar purification:
>
> - Precise visualization
> - Strong willpower
> - The capability of utmost concentration

The First Form of Nectar Purification ❖❖

Imagine your body as an empty vessel. It feels good as the white nectar flows from the object of meditation into this vessel and fills it until the liquid spills over on the top, taking with it all your physical and mental concerns and washing them away. All impurities are rinsed out through the openings in your upper body, such as your mouth, nose, and ears. Your body ends up fully cleansed.

Should you be burdened by negative influences on your mind—such as anger or intolerance—at the time of your meditation, you can focus on imagining the purification of these negative emotions.

Purification through the openings in your head is particularly effective in dealing with physical ailments in your upper body. If you wish to ease these problems, you can visualize the nectar cleaning intensively in those places and the impurities being washed away by the pure nectar that is flowing steadily over the rim of your body's vessel.

THE MEDITATION

Rest your hands loosely on your knees with the simple mudra of your palms facing upwards.

While the nectar is flowing into the vessel of your body, *inhale* slowly and gently and lift both hands sideways so they are on the same level with your eyes in a gesture of receiving the nectar (step one).

Now bring your hands toward your head (step two) and then back down to your lap with your palms facing down while you breathe *out* gently (step three). When you breathe in the next time, bring your hands up to the level of your eyes again (step four).

Mudra

Step One

Turn your palms outward now and push your hands upward in one motion, forming a beautiful arch. During this movement of pushing away, *exhale* gently and visualize your mental and physical transgressions washing away through the openings in your upper body (step five). When the exercise is completed, put your hands back down on your knees again with palms facing up. Finish this exercise as previously described on page 42.

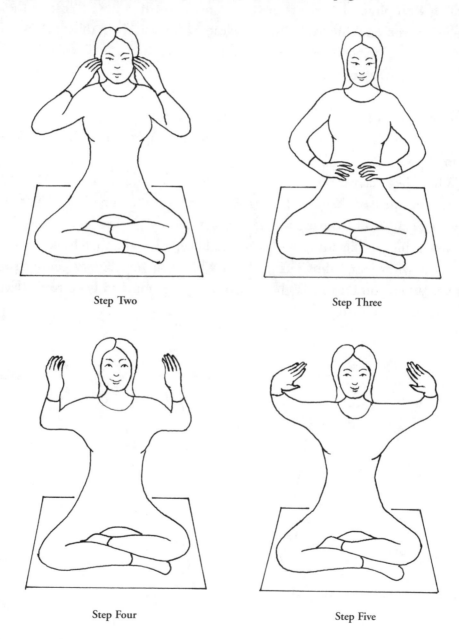

Step Two

Step Three

Step Four

Step Five

The Second Form of Nectar Purification ❖❖

In this second form of purification, the process takes place through the openings of your lower body. For this exercise, you will imagine your body to be a vessel with an opening at the pelvic chakra. You feel good as the white nectar flows from the object of meditation into your vessel, filling it to the top until it overflows, washing all your mental and physical transgressions out through the opening at the bottom of the vessel (your pelvic chakra). This thoroughly cleans your body. This particular purification is recommended at times when you suffer from ailments in the lower part of your body.

THE MEDITATION

Rest your hands loosely on your knees with the simple mudra of your palms facing up.

While the nectar is flowing into the vessel of your body, *inhale* slowly and gently and lift both hands sideways to be on the same level with your eyes in a gesture of receiving the nectar (step one).

Mudra

Step One

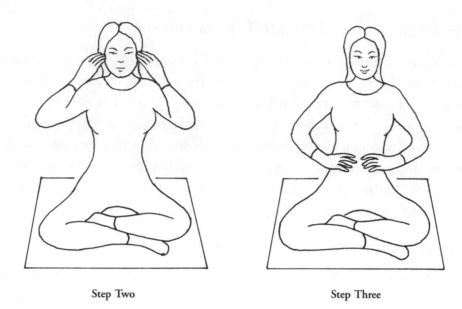

Step Two   Step Three

Bring your hands in toward your head (step two) and then down toward your lap with your palms facing down (step three). Push both hands away from your body with your palms facing out. During this movement of pushing away, *exhale* gently and visualize your mental and physical transgressions washing away through the openings in your lower body (step four). Rest your hands on your knees again with your palms facing up.

End this exercise as previously described on page 42.

Step Four

The Third Form of Nectar Purification ❖❖

This third form of nectar purification is very effective and particularly recommended in cases of serious illness.

Imagine the white nectar coming to you in the form of a powerful stream. It is comforting how the liquid runs into you and aims straight onto the ailing part of your body. The more intense and powerful your imagination, the more effective this exercise.

THE MEDITATION

Rest your hands loosely on your knees with the simple mudra of your palms facing up.

Inhale gently while the nectar streams into your body and lift both hands sideways to be on the same level with your eyes in a gesture of receiving the nectar (step one). Now bring your hands toward your head, then in the direction of the ailing part of your body with your palms facing down, then *exhale* (step two).

Mudra

Step One

Step Two

When you take your next breath, put both hands on the ailing spot (step three). Once there, turn the palms of your hands outward, then push both hands away from your body, with your palms also facing outward. During this movement of pushing away, *exhale* gently. At the same time, visualize in full devotion and complete confidence the powerful stream of white nectar destroying your illness (step four). Put your hands down to rest lightly on your knees with your palms facing up.

End this exercise as described previously on page 42.

Step Three

Step Four

NINE

The Ray-of-Light Purification

ANOTHER POPULAR FORM OF PURIFICATION IS the ray-of-light purification. It can be practiced on three levels: the Buddhist level, the level of people with different faiths, and the level of nonbelievers. Among Buddhists, the appropriate object of meditation for this cleansing exercise would again be the deity Vajra Sattva. Among Christians, Jesus or Mother Mary would be appropriate. People of different faiths can pick a holy being they are familiar with. An atheist can imagine the object in the form of a sunlike body of light that gives out a lot of healthy light and heat.

The special feature of this kind of purification is the effect that we experience from the object of meditation as an enormous source of energy filled with positive rays of light.

Start by doing the familiar preliminary actions for the meditation as described in the first part of this book. Review the seven elements in posture, as described previously on pages 18–21, if needed.

Now gather all your imagination to visualize your meditation object until it is fully present. Imagine the object to be illuminated with a warm source of light and slightly elevated from the ground. Originating from this overwhelming body of light is a cushioned ray of light that falls on you, covering your entire body, not unlike headlight beams.

These cozy, warming rays of light penetrate your entire body, including all its coarse and subtle substances, illuminating everything to every last corner of your body, including all mental and physical transgressions hiding there. You feel the rays of light in dark crevices where illness and bad emotional energy have been lodged up; you feel how the light intensifies in these places and how the penetrating rays of light extinguish the negative forces.

You feel fresh and invigorated and completely cleansed of all impurities.

Vajra Sattva Mantra (CD track 1)

For the ray-of-light purification, you can use the previously described Vajra Sattva mantra shown below and recited on the accompanying CD, track 1.

> *Om vajra sattva hum,*
> *om vajra sattva,*
> *mama vyadhi,*
> *vibend adi sarva,*
> *nishedak perbava,*
> *shantim kuru svaha.*

The Meditation

Rest your hands lightly on your knees with the simple mudra of your palms facing up. While bright and warm rays of light fall on you, *inhale* slowly and softly, then lift both hands to be on the same level with your eyes in a receiving gesture (step one).

Now bring your hands to your head and stroke down over it using the whole palms of your hands (step two). Stroke down over your face and your upper body (step three).

Mudra

Step One

Step Two

Step Three

While your hands are stroking down, *exhale* slowly and intently. While the insides of your hands are stroking down over your head, face, and upper body, imagine how the warming rays of light illuminate every dark corner of your body where physical and mental impurities are hiding (step four). When your palms reach your lap, turn them out and push your hands forward in an expelling motion (step five).

End the exercise by placing your hands gently back onto your knees with your palms facing up.

Step Four   Step Five

TEN

The Collection of Healing Power

THE MEDITATION CALLED the "collection of healing power" is beautiful, inspiring, and effective. Tibetans are convinced that nature harbors healing powers beyond estimation and that we can harness this power for our well-being using this particular meditation. This meditation is a way of taking advantage of the healing forces in nature. The collection-of-healing-power meditation is first recommended for physicians and healers to support their healing activities and to improve the effectiveness of the drugs they prescribe. In Tibetan tradition, this meditation is deemed to be of extra-precious value. It is also used for people who are ill to increase the effectiveness of the drugs they are taking, to speed their recovery, and to keep negative forces away from them.

The collection of healing power can be conducted on three different levels. A Buddhist will use the Medicine Buddha as the object of his or her meditation. This Buddha appears in bright sky-blue color; he symbolically carries in his left hand a beggar's bowl filled with essential healing powers. His right hand holds the medicinal plant called myrobalan. In Christianity, the figure of Jesus would be the closest to the Medicine Buddha. A secular practitioner might imagine a bright blue source of light that is saturated with comforting positive energy.

Overview

Begin with the customary preliminary actions for the meditation and focus on yourself for a moment.

Visualize the blue object of meditation with complete devotion. Do not stray from it. Start with your meditation when the object becomes clearly present.

Observe with your inner eye the way countless bright rays are developing, originating from the object of meditation, and going off in all ten directions: south, east, west, north, northeast, southeast, northwest, and southwest, as well as in the direction of the sky and the earth.

See how these rays are being nourished and how they absorb the healing forces of the earth, plants, trees, minerals, mountains, and oceans. They go off in all ten directions and then return to the object of meditation. From there, they flow into you in the form of beautifully fragrant bright rays of light that are saturated with healing power.

Now imagine how the warming and bright rays of light set out to work and destroy all your negative emotions, such as greed, hate, and ignorance, which are responsible for causing an imbalance among your bodily energies and are thus the source of many illnesses.

MEDICINE BUDDHA MANTRA (CD TRACK 2)

This Medicine Buddha mantra is used in Tibetan meditation to respectfully call upon the Medicine Buddha and ask him wholeheartedly for his blessings, so that one may be free from an ailment. This mantra is also whispered into the ear of a dying person to give reassurance. The Medicine Buddha mantra is recited on the accompanying CD, track 2.

> *Ta-dya-tha,*
> *om beishajye beishajye,*
> *maha beishajye beishajye,*
> *raja samungate svaha.*

IMPORTANT CONSIDERATIONS

The beginner should practice this meditation without the use of the following mudras. Only after you have become acquainted with the course of this meditation should you include the mudras. It is essential to remember to focus on deep and enthusiastic visualization. This is of particular importance with this exercise, in order to reap the most powerful effect in the collection of healing forces.

You have the option to let the mantra sink in by simply playing the CD instead of singing it yourself.

THE MEDITATION

Place your hands lightly on your knees with the simple mudra of your palms facing up. At the moment when the bright rays start flowing down onto you, bring your arms up slowly on the side of your body and *inhale* gently (step one).

When you *exhale* again, lift your head a little and bend your upper body forward; bring your arms to the front and pick up the healing forces of the earth and the oceans with your hands.

Mudra   Step One

Slowly straighten out your back again and let your arms follow the motion, keeping them angled in front of your abdomen while you *inhale* slowly and gently (step two). The palms of your hands face upward in a receiving gesture. As soon as your upper body has resumed its natural position, you again *exhale* gently (step three).

Step Two

Step Three

Step Four

Step Five

When you breathe *in* again, bring both arms up to the same level with your eyes and receive the healing powers of the trees and the plants while your palms are facing up. Then you breathe *out* gently.

With the following breath, raise your arms above your head and receive the healing forces of the mountains with your upward pointing palms. Then you *exhale* gently. Next you breathe *in* and bring your hands to your head, palms facing down (step four), and *exhale* gently while your hands sink down to your lap and rest lightly on your knees.

Your palms are facing up. During this moment, allow yourself to quietly absorb all forces (step five).

ELEVEN

Visualization of Breathing for Severe Mental and Physical Strain

THIS MEDITATION ON BREATHING is recommended at times of severe mental and physical strain. The exercise is intense and has an immediate effect.

MANTRA

Choose your own mantra from the accompanying CD and play it during the meditation.

Take up the customary posture for meditation after you are through with all your preliminaries for the meditation. Put your hands on your belly. *Inhale* gently through both nostrils. Try to bring as much air as possible into your lungs and sense with your hands how the abdominal area is arching slowly. Hold your breath for a moment (step one). *Exhale* through your mouth and slowly push out the air from your lungs, but forcefully and with purpose (step two).

Repeat this breathing routine, but alternate your action when you exhale by breathing out slowly and carefully one time and forcefully and with purpose the next. With each time you exhale strongly, you will feel relieved, relaxed, and loosened up.

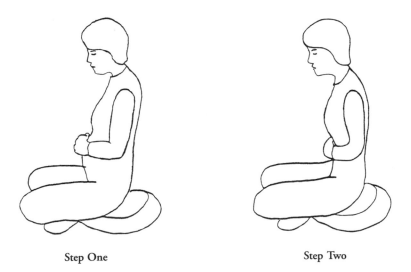

Step One   Step Two

- While slowly *inhaling* the air through the nose, into your lungs, and into your abdominal space, you create a profound sensation of absorbing an enormous amount of cleansing power in the form of fresh air.
- While *holding* your breath, imagine with all your might how this purifying energy enters every remote corner of your body and mind and thoroughly cleanses everything.
- While *exhaling* vigorously, you grow to be sincerely convinced that by the power of this exercise, all your mental and physical ailments are being transported out of your body for good.

Because your hands are resting on your abdomen while you do the exercise, you can feel how your hands rise with the intestinal cavity when you inhale, and how they fall when you exhale. Gentle pressure on your belly will help to press out every last bit of air.

TWELVE

Color Rain Showers

BECAUSE EVERY ACTION OF BODY and speech is dependent on the mind, and because an unhealthy state of mind will create suffering, it is of utmost importance that you take good care of your mind. A person in the West tends to be quite determined to take good care of his or her outer appearance—that is, the body. Tibetan meditation teaches us that it is just as important to regularly groom our inner appearance—that is, the mind. The meditation of color rain showers gives us the opportunity to groom our minds in a most comfortable manner.

This exercise will help you to keep negative emotions in check. In a further step, as described in Part Three, the exercises that are part of concentration and analytical meditation become necessary to completely overcome the emotions that cause suffering.

With the color rain showers, you visualize five colors. According to Tibetan meditation, each color is associated with a certain disposition of the mind that causes suffering; each color also has been assigned a purifying mantra. Each color, in the form of a rain cloud, has the ability to conquer one of these dispositions of the mind that causes suffering; furthermore, each color rain cloud has the power to purify your emotional state and free you from what is bothering you. You will find the associations in the table below. Depending on your present disposition, you can visualize the color that matches your feelings. It will not take you long to realize how a deep visualization of your chosen color has a direct influence on your emotions, and you will sense how the negative emotion disintegrates.

RAIN-CLOUD COLOR	EMOTION	MANTRA SYLLABLE
Blue	Desire	Ae
Green	Hate/Anger	Yam
White	Ignorance	Wam
Yellow	Pride	Lam
Red	Suspicion	Ram

COLOR RAIN SHOWER MANTRAS (CD TRACKS 3–7)

Recite the mantra that corresponds with the emotion you wish to cleanse from your mind. Each syllable shown in the table has a complete mantra that you recite in its long form. The recommended mantras can be found on the accompanying CD tracks 3 through 7.

Purification of Desire (CD track 3)
Om ah hum, ae *ho shutdi shudi a svaha.*

Purification of Anger and Hate (CD track 4)
Om ah hum, yam *ho shutdi shudi a svaha.*

Purification of Ignorance (CD track 5)

Om ah hum, wam *ho shutdi shudi a svaha.*

Purification of Pride (CD track 6)

Om ah hum, lam *ho shutdi shudi a svaha.*

Purification of Suspicion (CD track 7)

Om ah hum, ram *ho shutdi shudi a svaha.*

THE MEDITATION

Take up your customary position for meditation after you have done all preliminaries.

Depending on your present state of mind, your imagination will guide you and bring the particular rain-cloud color overhead that will help you to break down your present negative emotions. For example, at the times when your mind is troubled by desire, a trait that can cause suffering, you can bring upon yourself the blue rain cloud.

Begin slowly by imagining how this cloud above your head rains down on you in an evergrowing shower of blue color, engulfing you in a most agreeable manner. Sense how your desires that cause suffering abate gradually and how peace sets in again.

You would do the same exercise with a rain cloud of a different color, depending on the negative emotions that are bothering you at that moment.

THIRTEEN

Pooling the Energy of Five Elements

TIBETANS BELIEVE THAT THE WELL-BEING of body and mind is the key to a long and happy life. We can realize this ideal with the meditation on pooling the energy of five elements. This meditation is also considered to represent a form of the live-a-long-life meditation, and it can be practiced on three different levels. Buddhists visualize one of three deities during this meditation: Amitayus, in its red appearance; the White Tara; or Vijaya. For members of other religions, I recommend to visualize a deity or a holy being they feel particularly close to. While Jesus would be appropriate for people of Christian belief, nonbelievers can visualize a bright body of light with the property of indescribable strength.

According to Tibetan thinking, humans are made of the same five elements as nature itself: earth, water, fire, air, and space. These elements are associated with certain parts of the body. The element earth, symbolized by the color yellow, represents all solid parts of the body. The bodily fluids are tied with the element water, which is symbolized by the color white. Body heat originated in fire and is represented by the color red. Your breathing and nervous system are associated with wind or air, symbolized by the color green. The hollow spaces or cavities that are imbedded in our body are the element of space, which is represented by the color blue.

ELEMENT	MANTRA	CD TRACK	COLOR	BODY ASSOCIATION
Earth	Prithvi	8	Yellow	Bones, muscles, sinew, fat
Water	Utaka	9	White	Blood, body fluids
Fire	Agne	10	Red	Body heat
Wind/Air	Vayu	11	Green	Breathing and nervous system
Space	Akasha	12	Blue	Hollow spaces in the body

A harmonious balance between these five elements is the most important pre-requisite to a healthy body. When one of the elements is out of balance, this interference results in illness. Therefore, the Tibetans find it very important to maintain a healthy environment and consider it to be paramount to their survival. All of us are dependent on the well-functioning of the five elements.

Each and every one of the elements is necessary to keep our bodies functioning well and to contribute to a long life. To actualize this we need to clearly grasp the concept of the interconnectedness of the elements to awaken and strengthen our awareness of the importance of nature and the environment. Therefore, we should protect and conserve nature and all its precious forces.

The effect of the following meditation, which brings us close to nature, is based on the fact that intense meditation on the elements and their corresponding body parts helps us to regenerate. Our bodies are able to pick up plenty of power and energy through these meditations, and we can lay the foundation for a long and healthy life.

Take good care to conduct all preliminary actions for the meditation one after the other; enter your meditation by visualizing your object of meditation, which should be positioned at eye level. Stay with the object for a while.

To begin, observe white rays of light streaming from the object and going off in all directions, blending with the earth in order to gather its energy.

- To represent the color of the earth element, the rays of light change to yellow and return to the object of meditation, laden with the strength of the earth. Every single beam of yellow light floods your object of meditation and reflects onto you in order to become one with your body. Try to experience this moment of unification with the yellow beams, which carry the energy of the earth, with a conscious mind. Notice how you have been invigorated by this power.
- Next you experience more rays of light emerging from the meditation object, which, in succession, will go out to harness the energy of the other elements.
- The strength of the water element will return beams of white color to your object of meditation.
- The strength of fire reflects rays of red color.
- The strength of the wind or air returns beams of green color.
- The strength of space brings about rays of blue, which first engulf the object of meditation and then come down on you, who have been blessed with the harmonic balance of the forces of the five elements.

Let yourself be invigorated in body and mind and be happy. You are convinced that all obstacles to a long and healthy life have now been eradicated.

If you would like to intensify the gathering of energy, you can conduct the corresponding exercises and use the associated mantras. The basic body position is the same as for the first three exercises. When you have finished all five elements, you have the option to close with one of the mantras for long life (see page 78).

Gathering the Energy of the Earth Element ❖❖

MANTRA TO POOL THE ENERGY OF EARTH (CD TRACK 8)
Om sarva prithvi *perbava samgriha bavate svaha.*

Stand in a relaxed fashion with your legs straight and your feet at shoulder's width apart (step one). When you *exhale* now, bend your upper body forward while keeping your head up slightly in order to form a straight line with your spine. While you are slowly bending forward, let your arms dangle freely (step two).

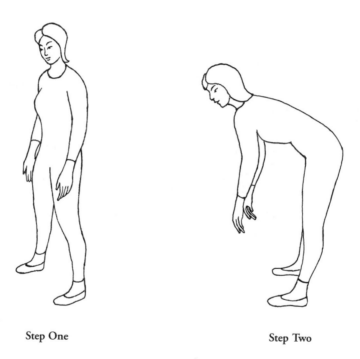

Step One   Step Two

Feel the light tension in your legs. As soon as you have come to the lowest point of your bow, bend your knees a little and let your head hang loosely (step three).

Now touch the ground with your fingertips and pick up the energy of the earth with both hands while you straighten out again slowly and simultaneously *inhale* slowly and gently (step four). Let your behind sag a little now and take care to align your upper body in a natural upright position. With your palms facing up, bring your hands level with your eyes (step five).

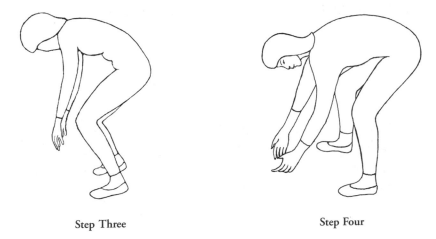

Step Three   Step Four

Turn your palms over to direct away from your face. Hold your breath for a
moment and then push both hands down gently to the same level with your
stomach (step six).

Step Five   Step Six

Step Seven   Step Eight

Move them apart and let them hang loosely on your sides again. Your knees are still bent slightly (step seven). Only when you are completely finished with the exercise, straighten out your legs again (step eight).

Gathering the Energy of the Water Element ❖❖

MANTRA TO POOL THE ENERGY OF WATER (CD TRACK 9)
Om sarva utaka *perbava samgriha bavate svaha.*

Stand in a relaxed fashion with your legs straight and your feet at shoulder's width apart (step one). When you *exhale,* bend your upper body forward while keeping your head up slightly in order to form a straight line with your spine. While you are slowly bending forward, let your arms dangle freely (step two).

As soon as you have come to the lowest point of your bow, bend your knees a little and let your head hang loosely. Now use both hands to form a kind of vessel by cupping them. Imagine how you dip your hands into crystal clear water, and lift up its renewing energy with your hands (step three).

Bring your hands, filled with that water, up above your head and, at the

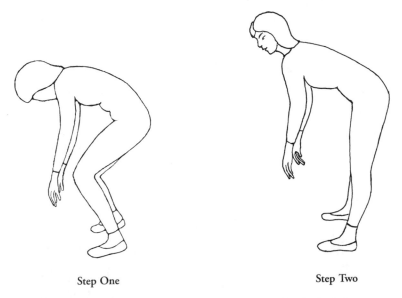

Step One   Step Two

same time, straighten your body out again (step four). While you are coming up, *inhale* again, slowly and gently. Let your behind sag a little now and take care to align your upper body in a natural upright position.

Step Three   Step Four

Hold your breath for a moment and then, with your imagination, let the water run down over your body while you *exhale,* then use the inside of your hands to stroke over your head and face (step five). Next let your hands drop gently to your sides again. Your knees are still bent slightly (step six).

Straighten out your legs only when you are completely finished with the exercise (step seven).

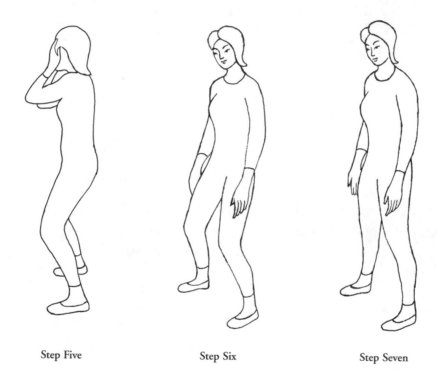

Step Five   Step Six   Step Seven

Gathering the Energy of the Fire Element ❖❖

MANTRA TO POOL THE ENERGY OF FIRE (CD TRACK 10)

Om sarva agne *perbava samgriha bavate svaha.*

Stand in a relaxed fashion with your legs straight and your feet at shoulder's width apart (step one). When you *exhale* now, slowly bend your upper body while keeping your head up slightly in order to form a straight line with your spine (step two).

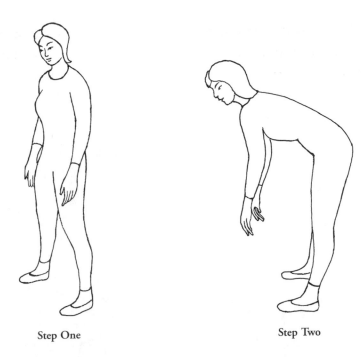

Step One   Step Two

While you are slowly bending forward, let your arms dangle freely. As soon as you have come to the lowest point of your bow, bend your knees a little and let your head hang loosely. Now touch the ground with the tips of your fingers and imagine how you absorb a great amount of the warming energy of fire and how you use it to enhance your well-being (step three).

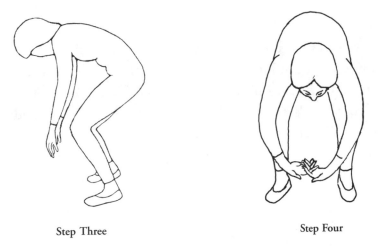

Step Three   Step Four

Bring your palms into a position facing up, spread your fingers, and interlock them. Visualize your fingers in this interlocked position as they symbolize fire and its comforting heat (step four). Take your hands up to be on the same level with your heart. At the same time, slowly straighten out again. While you are coming up, *inhale* slowly and gently. Let your behind sag a little now and take care to align your upper body in a natural upright position. *Exhale* gently and slowly (step five).

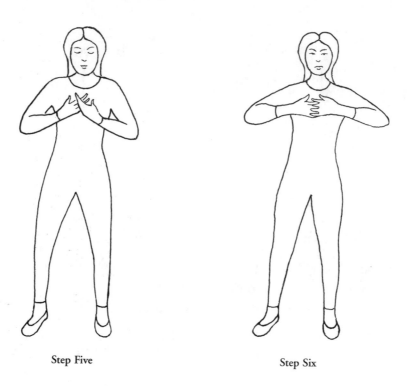

Step Five   Step Six

Inhale slowly again with your palms facing your body, loosening them somewhat. Keeping them interlocked, place them down on your chest. Hold your breath and let the heat of the fire warm you (step six). When you *exhale* again, take your hands apart and let them drop gently to your sides again. Your knees are still bent slightly (step seven).

Only when you are completely finished with the exercise, straighten out your legs (step eight).

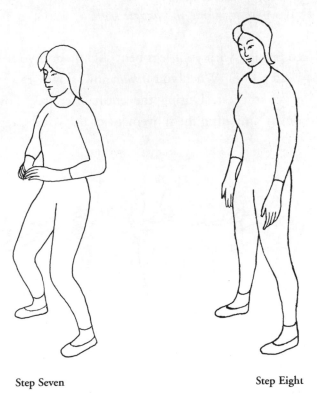

Step Seven   Step Eight

Gathering the Energy of the Wind Element ❖ ❖

MANTRA TO POOL THE ENERGY OF WIND (CD TRACK 11)
Om sarva vayu *perbava samgriha bavate svaha.*

Stand in a relaxed fashion with your legs bent slightly and your feet at shoulder's width apart (step one). When you *inhale* now, slowly raise your straight arms in front of your chest. During the entire exercise, move all fingers quickly up and down, imitating the movement of the wind (step two).

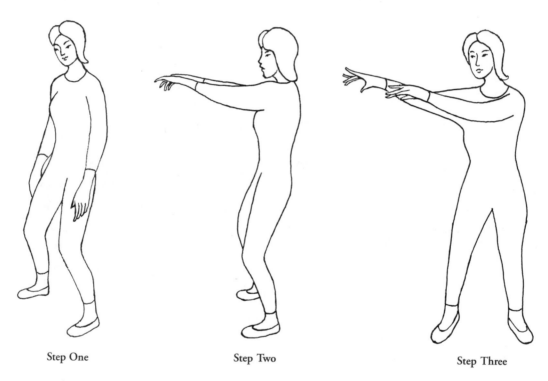

Step One   Step Two   Step Three

The next time you *exhale,* swing both arms to the right and shift your body weight over to the right leg. Then both arms swing back to the middle while you *inhale* slowly and gently (step three).

When you *exhale* again, swing your arms to the left and shift your body weight evenly onto your left leg, and when you *inhale* now, bring the arms back to the middle so your body weight is distributed evenly over both legs (step four). Put both hands on your abdominal area when you *exhale* now, and there absorb the energy of the wind (step five).

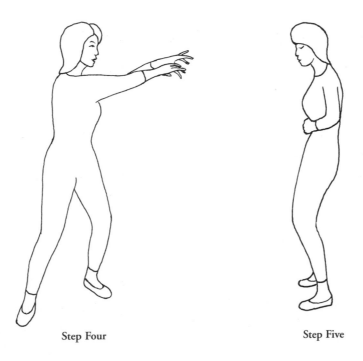

Step Four   Step Five

Inhale again, take your hands off your belly, and finish the exercise by turning your hands downward. *Exhale* with purpose while you push your hands down and let them sink to your sides (step six).

Straighten out your legs to complete the exercise (step seven).

Step Six

Step Seven

Gathering the Energy of the Space Element ❖❖

MANTRA TO POOL THE ENERGY OF SPACE (CD TRACK 12)

Om sarva akasha *perbava samgriha bavate svaha.*

Stand in a relaxed fashion with your legs bent slightly and your feet at shoulder's width apart (step one). When you *inhale* now, slowly raise your arms sideways and bring them up to your forehead where your hands meet in the symbolic gesture representing the energy of the element space: Spread the fingers of both hands and bring them together slowly until the fingertips touch, forming a hollow structure (step two).

The next time you *exhale,* bring this symbol of space across the middle of your chest and down to your lap. Then you *inhale* and turn your hands so the thumbs are on top and hold your breath for a moment (step three).

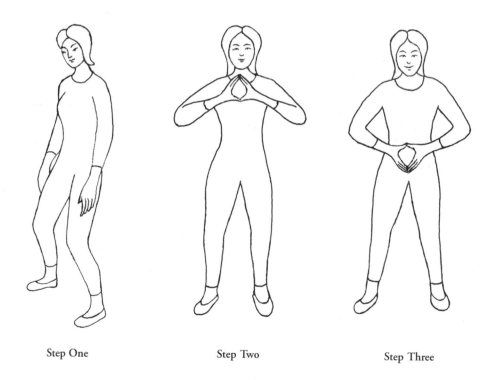

Step One   Step Two   Step Three

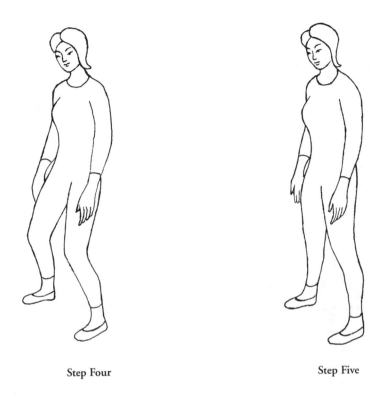

Step Four   Step Five

When you *exhale* again, take your hands apart, turning them downward, and let them sink to your sides (step four).

When you are completely finished with the exercise, straighten out your legs (step five).

Finish with the mantras for long life

The meditations on the pooling of the five elements can be ended with the following three long-life mantras. After you have completed the five exercises to gather energy as described previously, sit down on your cushion in a comfortable position and choose one of the following mantras. Play the CD recording of your chosen mantra and allow it to gently take effect on you. It is up to you which of the three you wish to use and whether you wish to sing along. Tibetans believe that a long life is a wonderful present, because it provides them with the opportunity to accumulate as many good deeds as possible and to create a better karma for themselves. Long-life mantras have therefore a direct influence on extending your own life.

AMITAYUS MANTRA (CD TRACK 13)

The mantra below is a respectful invocation to the deity Amitayus and asks to bless us with a long life.

> *Om ama rani jivente svaha.*

TARA MANTRA (CD TRACK 14)

This is the mantra to respectfully call upon the deity Tara and ask her—the savior—to guard us and liberate us from all obstacles in this and in our future lives.

> *Om tare tut-tare ture svaha,*
> *om tare tu-tare,*
> *ture mama ayu punye,*
> *geyana,*
> *pushtim kuru svaha.*

VIJAYA DEVI MANTRA (CD TRACK 15)

The focus of this mantra, which addresses the deity Vijaya, is a sincere request to be blessed with immortality.

> *Om drum svaha,*
> *om amrita ayurdate svaha.*

FOURTEEN

Igniting the Inner Fire

THE MEDITATION TO IGNITE THE INNER FIRE is an exercise adapted from traditional Tumo or Tschendralin practice. In Tibetan Buddhism, this is considered one of the most secret Tantric techniques. It is a special method to gain enlightenment.

The effectiveness of this method has been proven objectively. Physiological measurements have been taken on yogis using this type of meditation to ignite their inner fire (*tumo* in Tibetan or *chandali* in Sanscrit). The meditation enabled them to remain outdoors all night with no clothing and in ice-cold conditions. They were even able to dry towels that had been dipped in cold water and used to cover them for the purposes of the experiment.

The proof of this phenomenon does not signify, of course, that the yogis ignited a real fire inside themselves. Instead, it was the energy of their precise visualization, their immense concentration, and their strong willpower that caused this phenomenon. Their body temperature had increased measurably.

The following exercise was developed with traditional chandali meditation in mind but does not copy it; therefore, we can not expect the same level of effect previously the described yogis experienced.

In Buddhist tradition, the chandali practice is considered to be among the highest levels of perfection possible; it demands the practicing student to take, without exception, all prior steps necessary for the meditation and that he or she previously has done these steps under the guidance of an experienced teacher.

My own experiences with this meditation have encouraged me, however, to make this exercise accessible to students in the West by adapting it from the one that brings about this highest form of perfection. Even though you will not be able to raise your body temperature using this exercise, you will still experience a pronounced feeling of joy and happiness contributing to your general well-being.

For you to understand the origin of this effect, you should become familiar with the function of the subtle body.

The subtle body

According to Tibetan reasoning, humans have not only their material body but also a subtle one. Thousands of wide and narrow channels connect both kinds of bodies. Our eyes are unable to see these channels that constantly carry the "wind [lung in Tibetan] that keeps us alive." This lung is inseparable from our consciousness, comparable to the *prana* in Hindi yoga systems and the *ch'i* in Chinese acupuncture philosophy.

There are three main channels: the central channel, the left channel, and the right channel. Their beginning point is located between a person's eyebrows. From there, they run upward to the crown chakra. The passage then parallels the spine, running through all seven chakras—the centers of subtle energy—and ending about two inches below the belly button. A chakra has been described as a wheel or a disc, a place where many of these interwoven channels come together and form a knot in the shape of a circle.

Do not visualize all seven main chakras during the following meditation; instead, concentrate on the crown chakra, the throat chakra, the heart chakra, and the navel chakra. See the image on page 81 for the location of the chakras.

At conception, our "life-sustaining wind" starts running through the side channels. The central channel remains passive. Tibetan Buddhism's ideas about subtle energies teach and explain that the activity in the side channels triggers situations that cause negative states of mind. By practicing the meditations taught in the ancient Buddhist scriptures, a person can maneuver the life-supporting wind into the central channel and thus phase out the activity in the side channels, thereby enhancing the effect of a positive state of mind. In other words, this implies that we are unable to gain complete happiness as long as these life-supporting winds are still flowing through both side channels.

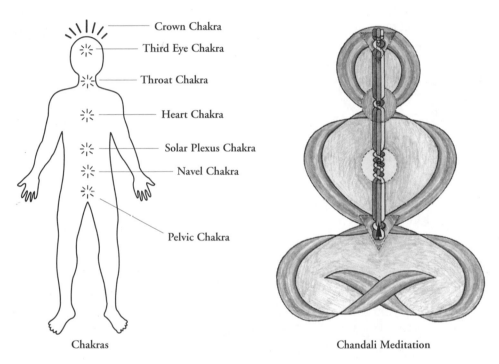

Crown Chakra

Third Eye Chakra

Throat Chakra

Heart Chakra

Solar Plexus Chakra

Navel Chakra

Pelvic Chakra

Chakras   Chandali Meditation

In the Chandali Meditation image (above right), you can observe how the side channels form a reclining figure eight, enclosing the central channel near the location of the chakras. The currents of the positive winds, which are only found in the central channel, are still being blocked in the area of the chakras. By practicing the chandali technique, you have the opportunity to untie these knots and consciously guide the winds into the central passage where the pure and positive winds can flow freely; this is a prerequisite for experiencing the wonder of complete bliss.

The chandali practice is a very advanced form of meditation; therefore, I recommend that you try the simplified version first.

Preliminary Meditation One ❖❖

Start by going through the preparatory steps for a meditation. When you feel relaxed and calm, express your determination to do the following exercise with all your heart. Concentrate and then visualize your own body as an empty vessel.

In the next step, visualize with all your might the three main channels originating between your eyebrows and running parallel to each other, first upward to the crown of your head and then immediately in front of your spine downward to a point two inches below your navel. This is the spot where the side channels hook up and lead into the central channel. Imagine these channels as tubes; exact visualization of the colors is of utmost importance.

- The outer walls of the central channel are blue, but the inside walls are red.
- The walls of the channel to the right are red.
- The walls of the channel to the left are white.

Take all the time you need to make sure that this image appears clearly and solidly before your inner eye.

At this point, visualize the four chakras: the first on the same level with your navel, the second on the same plane as your heart, and the next two by your throat and in the crown of your head.

Before you delve into the main meditation to spark your inner fire, you need to loosen the knots that have built up around the chakras. The following meditation will make this possible.

Preliminary Meditation Two:
Releasing the Entanglement in the Central Channel ❖❖

After the first preliminary meditation, create in your mind a shiny white droplet of liquid with a red tinge in the central channel of your heart chakra. This powerful droplet now rises slowly from your heart chakra to your crown chakra. From there it drops down to the origin of the channels between your eyebrows and then moves gradually back up to the crown and then down again, past the heart chakra to the navel chakra.

Let this white droplet repeat this journey, up and down, three times. On the third repetition, bring the droplet back to your heart chakra to transform it into the heart droplet, which represents the energy of bliss.

The knotted channels around the chakras loosen up through the up-and-down motion of the droplet and thus create a smooth passage for other droplets to glide up and down the channels. With this you have fulfilled all prerequisites for the main meditation of the sparking of the inner fire. I recommend that you take a break and relax a little before you proceed.

Meditation on Igniting the Inner Fire ❖❖❖

After you have allowed yourself a little relaxation time, invoke the image that you visualized during the preliminary meditation and concentrate on holding that image while creating a new droplet on each of the three upper chakras in the central channel.

- The droplet on the crown chakra is white.
- The droplet on the throat chakra is red.
- The droplet on the heart chakra is blue.

Next visualize a thornlike object on the navel chakra, which has the potential of fire. This object is called *athung;* it is pointed on the top and widens at the bottom and is known to be the main trigger mechanism for lighting the inner fire. The drawing on page 81 will help you with the visualization.

While your focus now is inseparable from the athung, breathe in very, very slowly and gently through your nose. Let your breath flow into the side channels and travel their full length until it reaches the spot below the navel chakra, where the side channels lead into the central channel.

Then bring your breath back up onto the navel chakra and use your imagination to heat up the athung; this will activate the power of fire in it and generate a lot of heat.

Exhale very slowly through your nose again.

Repeat this exercise a second time. By the power of your intense visualization, you are able to make the athung glow.

Repeat this exercise for a third time and devote all possible energy to this task. Thus, you will be able to cause the athung to catch fire. A narrow intense flame will develop pointing upward.

Once you have created it, use the flame when you *inhale* the next time to warm up the droplets on the crown, throat, and heart chakras. The strong heat coming from the flame will dissolve the white droplet in the crown chakra, and its essence, the energy of bliss, will fall onto the throat chakra and unite with the red droplet. At this point, when the white droplet blends with the red one, you experience a warm sensation of happiness.

Then this blended droplet starts to dissolve and falls down onto the heart chakra where it combines with the blue droplet.

During this process of blending, you will experience an even stronger sensation of happiness. Now the blue droplet starts melting and falls, together with the other essences, down onto the navel chakra; all three droplets are united now in this location.

This blending creates even greater happiness than you felt beforehand and, in a climax, the essence falls onto the athung flame, which has the effect of pouring oil into a fire; the heat intensifies and the flame gets warmer.

This unusual and comforting heat penetrates your entire body—the part consisting of coarse matter as well as the subtle body—and fills it with an overwhelming feeling of inner bliss and joy.

Important considerations

In case you are not used to this kind of visualization, take ample time to get to know it well. It is important that you master the first step before moving on to the next one. Be aware of the fact that in doing this particular meditation, you must, without exception, have met the following requirements:

- Precise visualization ability
- Strong willpower
- Utmost ability to concentrate

FIFTEEN

The Pure Land

FOR THIS MEDITATION ON THE PURE LAND, you imagine a pure place such as paradise—a kingdom where you will go after you die. Buddhists believe that most deities have a "pure land" of their own. The moment a person dies, the deity with whom he or she has had the closest relationship and sought for spiritual shelter has a certain influence. It has been said that the angel-like beings of the pure land of that certain deity will come and guide the dying or dead person to that particular paradise with lovely music and song. This is where the dying person can separate from life on earth in complete peace and happiness.

In Christianity the "pure land" is represented by the kingdom of God, with its angels and heavenly sounds. Depending on your belief system, you will have particular ideas about what that place could be like. Let yourself be guided by your own creativity. Most important, remember that the pure land has nothing but excellent properties.

For the living, this kind of visualization has the primary purpose of achieving a wonderful feeling of happiness. Do this exercise at times when you are not feeling so well, when you are down. In particular, people who suffer from depression will find this meditation helpful to regain a glimpse of light and to step out of the darkness of depression.

In spiritual terms, this visualization of the pure land serves as an exercise to prepare a person to be able to die consciously. When it has been practiced, it becomes much easier to bring about the images of the pure land in the hour of death. As you will see from the following explanation, the meditation to transfer the mind into the pure land is of great importance to a spiritual person at the time of death.

Visualizing the Pure Land ❖

The meditation that visualizes the pure land is not dependent on time or space. You can do it anywhere, at any moment. You may be sitting down on a bench, on a walk, on a bus, or even lying on a beach. You may think, for example, of a wonderful and beautiful landscape with snow-covered mountains, a meadow filled with fragrant flowers in bloom, crystal-clear lakes, or a place where the renewing ocean waves break on a white beach strewn with palm trees.

Imagine yourself lingering in this pure place. People free from any physical or mental problems surround you; they are not suffering any harm and are full of serene joyfulness. It is a location where you are completely happy in body and soul, a place you like to think about and always wish to return to.

Transfer of Consciousness to the Pure Land:
The Gentle Phowa Practice to Help the Dying ❖❖❖

Have you ever paid attention to how much time you spend making plans and preparing for your future? I have noticed that Western children learn at an early age to prepare well for all kinds of situations, such as for school, for their spare time, and for vacations. Every detail is considered and nothing is left to chance.

In Tibet, people are more concerned to prepare very well for the most important journey they will ever take—the spiritual one through death. We like to prepare well for small and big trips and think of everything we possibly may need; therefore, we should also be very well prepared for our last journey.

Everybody has to die sooner or later; this is a natural phenomenon. Many people are very afraid of death—understandably so. This fear, however, can be of great hindrance in the moment of dying because the mind experiences restlessness and is at a loss. None of us can choose our moment of death or how it will take place. It may happen suddenly and without warning; for example, there may be an accident, a stroke, or a heart attack. In most cases, there is a prolonged illness that precedes death and the person experiences a dwindling of his or her strength. Great pain and sadness come over the dying person—and his or her relatives and friends. Helplessness and, in some cases, panic can interfere severely with the desired peacefulness of the dying individual.

However, people who, while still in good health, become familiar with the visualization of the pure land—the place they wish to live after their death—will find it easier to remember it during the time when they are about to die. The visualization of the pure land is therefore very important, as is the meditation on the transfer of consciousness of the mind to the pure land. It prepares you to die consciously and peacefully.

The valuable guidelines in this section are called *phowa* in the Tibetan language, which means the transformation or transfer of the spirit. Experienced Tantric practitioners who did not manage to reach enlightenment in their lifetime use the phowa. They practice the meditation in order to take advantage of the hour of their death; to help themselves, aided by powerful means, transfer their spirit to the pure land where they will continue with their exercises. People of different belief systems all have their own ideas about a pure land. It is important that you are able to imagine what that paradise is like, that you know about it beforehand, and that it is the place you wish to escape to.

The phowa technique is extraordinary because not only people that are initiated in secret Tantric practices are allowed to use it, but also ordinary Buddhists. A person who practices the phowa is able to implement it for his or her own needs and can, with great benefit, apply it to other people by helping them through it when they are dying.

The phowa practice is known to be one of the most powerful means to transfer the spirit of a person to a stage of higher consciousness. Therefore, it only may be exercised under the strict supervision of an experienced teacher.

I will introduce you to a gentle form of phowa that follows the traditional practice, but that can be used by anyone, without concern about dangerous consequences. I provide some pointers on how to remain still and calm as you peacefully embark on your journey to another existence in the moment of your death.

This meditation, as many of the others, can also be performed on three levels: Buddhists visualize the deity Amitabha. This deity has been said to have a special relationship to our earthly world. For instance, Amitabha told the deity Chenrezi to send all living beings on this planet (Zambuling in Tibetan) to the pure land of Amitabha. People of other creeds may choose a well-known, enlightened holy being who is part of their belief system. Christians can visualize Jesus during this exercise, and atheists, again, can envision a body of light charged with enormous positive energy.

Today many people are convinced that death can be compared with the snuffing of the flame on a candle. This view has the potential to trigger great despair and sadness, because the person settles for being left in eternal darkness after death, with nothing to look forward to. Under any circumstances, it would be preferable to die with hopeful and positive expectations than to die without hope and depressed. Therefore, I recommend rehearsing the meditation on the transfer of the mind into pure land, despite one's beliefs.

How to do the exercise

Perform all preliminary exercises in preparation for a deeply involved session.

Following the Chandali meditation technique, imagine your body as an empty vessel, only this time visualize merely the central channel—blue on the outside wall and red on the inside—as it runs from the navel chakra up to the crown of your head. The opening at the bottom of the channel is closed with a moon-shaped disk and is smaller than the opening at the crown level because the channel widens from the bottom to the top. The drawing on page 89 will help you to visualize the image.

The object of meditation that you chose earlier is visualized in all its glory now, positioned on top of the opening of that channel located by your crown; the bottom of the channel is resting comfortably on a soft flower cushion.

Now turn your attention to the beginning point of the central channel where you visualize a shiny white and shimmering droplet the size of a pea. This droplet is as soft and light as a cotton ball, yet at the same time, it has the springiness of a ball that is well inflated.

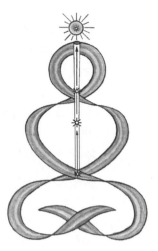

Gentle Phowa Practice

Allow your mind to blend and become one with this shimmering white droplet. Generate a boundless deep desire to unite with the object of meditation, which is positioned on top of the opening of the central channel, so you can enter the pure land of your dreams together.

AMITABHA MANTRA (CD TRACK 16)
Accompany your great desire by allowing the following Amitabha mantra, found on CD track 16, to sink into your innermost place.

Om ami daba hri.

After you have empowered your desire by reciting the mantra, proceed with the exercise.

While thoroughly fused with the white droplet, you begin the slow journey up the central channel. You have a strong sensation of exceptionally beautiful emotions of love and joy while you become one with the object of meditation, which radiates bright light in its position above the opening by your crown. You are then taken to the pure land. Disembark from the object of meditation and step into the wonderful pure land that you already know from past visualizations. Stay there for a while to absorb the heavenly energy.

Return to the object of meditation for it to carry you back. Above the opening by your crown, separate from the object and slowly climb down the central channel until you land softly on the flower cushion at the beginning of the channel. Consciously linger in that place for moment and then rise again.

You may repeat this exercise between three and twenty-one times. I recommend that you perform this gentle phowa practice regularly for it to be easily accessible in the actual moment of dying.

You can end the gentle phowa practice with the following long-life mantras. Depending on your need, you may use just one or all four mantras.

VAJRA GURU MANTRA (CD TRACK 19)

Om ah hum vajra guru padme siddhi hum.

AMITAYUS MANTRA (CD TRACK 13)

Om ama rani jivente svaha.

VIJAYA DEVI MANTRA (CD TRACK 15)

Om drum svaha, om amrita ayurdate svaha.

TARA MANTRA (CD TRACK 14)

Om tare tut-tare ture svaha,
om tare tut-tare,
ture mama ayu punye,
geyana,
pushtim kuru svaha.

Bringing About Courage: Preparing for Your Own Death and Helping Others Who Are Dying ❖❖❖

If you wish to produce courage, it is best to start out by accepting the nature of impermanence with regard to all things and phenomena, including your own person.

The exercise on pages 131–136 will help you to understand this context. It is perfectly normal that people are afraid of the unknown and that they prefer to avoid dealing with death rather than getting to learn more about it. To prepare well for your own death, however, requires you to look the truth in the eye instead of shying away from it. Every living being on this earth has been born to die sooner or later, and it dies to be born again. This law of nature applies to all living creatures, man or animal, rich or poor, weak or strong. A person who is aware of this cycle will be able to transform his or her fears into courage. That person doesn't merely help his or her cause but also is able to help and provide courage to those who are seriously ill or dying.

When a person passes from this life in dignity, it is not only comforting to the person dying but also relieves the sadness and pain of the ones left behind. In regard to death, we ought not to neglect our ability to make plans and to prepare for all kinds of occasions. Tibetans are very careful to not leave debts when they are about to die in order to avoid unnecessarily burdening people that are left behind. Writing up a will in a timely manner to divide up everything you own will help your mind to separate from things of material value. With the moment of death approaching, it is best for the mind to be free of all material notions. In addition, no negative feelings should be weighing on the mind. Encourage the dying person to let go of any negative physical or emotional ballast and remind him or her to create love and compassion toward others instead.

The mind of the dying person needs to be free of any burden, according to Buddhist concept, so that the person can take the journey into the pure land without any obstacles in his or her path. Without these elements in place, a person will resemble a bird whose foot has been tied to a rock. He or she would be unable to get away without being freed from the load.

If a dying person has previously studied the different techniques of meditation, read to him or her the instructions for the meditation on love and compassion (page 142) as well as the meditation on emptiness (page 126) so he or she will find it easier to concentrate.

According to Tibetan Buddhist views, people should not be crying in the presence of the dying person if it can be avoided, because it would be disturbing the concentration of the one who is dying. Instead, mourners are encouraged to stroke the dying person lovingly and, speaking softly, relate details about the journey to the pure land: Angelic beings are awaiting his or her arrival in this place with heavenly music and songs. These angelic beings will be present to receive and accompany the person to his or her deity. You can also whisper the Medicine Buddha mantra (page 54, CD track 2) into the person's ear.

It is mostly important—and not only among Tibetans—to reassure the dying person not to worry about the ones who are mourning.

Peace and quiet during this phase of dying helps the person to concentrate on the meditation on the transfer of the mind to the pure land that was practiced in his or her lifetime and to do the exercise without disturbance. It is very helpful to have a spiritual friend nearby who also is familiar with this practice and can remind the dying person of the different steps to take during the meditation.

In case the dying person is not familiar with the gentle phowa practice, you can do the exercise for him or her by visualizing the central channel of the dying person instead of your own. Use both your hands to gently take the hands of the dying person so he or she can sense your love and compassion. In that position, do the gentle phowa practice together slowly, concentrated, and without interruption.

Every one of us is capable of assisting a dying person in taking the gentle and peaceful journey to another place of being, even without experience in applicable meditations or knowledge of the gentle phowa practice, by observing the following types of conduct:

- Make the dying person feel at home and cared for.
- Talk gently and give out warmth by holding hands and gentle stroking.
- Reassure the dying person that he or she is not alone and that you are there solely for his or her well-being.
- Convince the dying person that you want to keep him or her company.
- Read from a spiritual text if the dying person so wishes.
- Regardless of the dying person's creed, you can play any of the following mantras from the accompanying CD.

> Vajra Guru Mantra (CD track 19)
> Chenrezi Mantra (CD track 17)
> Tara Mantra (CD track 14)
> Medicine Buddha Mantra (CD track 2)
> Vijaya Devi Mantra (CD track 15)
> Vajra Sattva Mantra (CD track 1)

PART THREE

*Meditations on Overcoming
the Origins of Suffering*

PART TWO OF THIS BOOK INTRODUCED YOU TO the meditations on relieving suffering; I now would like you to become familiar with meditations that take a deeper look into the origins of suffering, the sources responsible for all symptoms of suffering as have been previously described.

The instructions that follow are based on the traditions of Tibetan meditation and will help you to understand the fundamental origins of suffering. Before being able to fully grasp the sources of suffering, it is necessary to comprehend the function and nature of the mind.

Function and nature of the mind

The mind completely lacks matter; nor does it have any physical form. By nature it is clear, pure, without blemish, and, according to Tibetan Buddhism, it has Buddha Nature potential, which is the true, unchangeable, and eternal nature of all beings. All living beings—including animals—are equipped with this precious Buddha Nature and, because it is present in every creature, each has the potential to realize Buddhahood and enlightenment.

When left to its own devices, the activity of the mind is limited, as is the performance of a king who has been deserted by everyone in his kingdom. In this context, the Tibetan training of the mind recognizes three gates: body, speech, and mind. Body and speech doggedly follow the mind without fail; they do as they are told. The behavior of the body and speech can have far-reaching consequences. Watch yourself during everyday situations and notice how the state of your mind has control over your speech and body and how it expresses itself. Practice new types of behavior that are guided by patience and tolerance and observe the reaction of your fellow humans. If you speak gently, for example, and match this with appropriate gestures and facial expressions, you will find that people start turning to you, and that you are making friends. On the other hand, you will find that if you speak harshly and use threatening body language, people will turn away from you—you are making enemies.

Indeed, this behavior of the two gates will determine war or peace in this world. The instructions the mind passes on to its two henchmen, body and speech, depend entirely on its condition. When content and full of harmony, the mind will relate instructions that are beneficial and useful for everyone. A state of mind that is influenced by confusion, dissatisfaction, or aggression sends instructions of a dangerous nature, which cause great harm. At the same time, the mind does not realize how this harm will cause this suffering that, in return, will reflect onto the mind itself, causing still more suffering.

> A mind that causes harm, sooner or later, will be suffering the most from those consequences—this fact may be realized in this life or in a later one.

The mind needs its followers, body and speech, in order to be effective. The action of the mind, then, is directly connected with the three poisons, or entanglements: hate, greed, and ignorance. Once the three poisons have successfully captivated the mind, the mind produces the root causes for suffering. It ceases to be itself and is merely ordered about by the three kinds of poison. The mind changes constantly; at times, it is happy and friendly, and then it is depressed and deceitful. Sometimes it will behave like a friendly person who has lost his or her original personality due to the abuse of alcohol and who lets go of any self-control. Or it may behave like a light bulb that doesn't give out much light because it is covered with dirt. Analogous to the dirt that momentarily reduces the output of the light bulb, the three negative entanglements—hate, greed, and ignorance—obscure the mind.

According to Tibetan thinking, the true nature of the mind is free of any negativity and is the nature of Buddha in us. Our state of mind can be obscured by the three kinds of poison and, in the process, becomes wild and unpredictable.

It is a most precious virtue of the mind to possess the infinite ability and willingness to learn. Tibetan meditation takes advantage of this virtue, and it can teach numerous different techniques to tame and educate the mind. Start by looking upon the mind as a roaming, wild creature, always on the run, which has to be captured at any cost. We shall try to harness our wild mind like a mustang that must be tamed before it can become useful to us.

Just as people have various methods and tricks to tame horses, so the Tibetan school of higher mental training and meditation has a number of helpful means to tame the mind, such as analytical and concentration meditation.

SIXTEEN

Concentration Meditation

❖ ❖ ❖

THE GOAL IN CONCENTRATION MEDITATION is to develop the ability to concentrate on any kind of object without being distracted and to maintain and stabilize this state of concentration. For this reason, this type of meditation is also called "placement" or "calm-abiding" meditation. All your concentration is pointed at the object at hand. Developing this ability is the most important component of this meditation. It also acts as a preliminary exercise for analytical meditation, which helps you to investigate the true nature of an object and, in a deeper thought process, explore the origins of suffering. Both methods, the concentration as well as the analytical meditation, are necessary to do this. Using analytical meditation alone, you will not be able to explore the sources of suffering and its most important features. Doing so would be the equivalent of trying to view a beautiful painting with the help of a flickering candle in an otherwise dark room. If, however, you start out by fixing the candle to allow it to burn steadily, you create the conditions to study the painting carefully.

This method will teach you to reach a level of concentration that will be of additional support to you when you do the exercises that I introduced in the previous part of the book. Your sessions of meditation on relieving suffering will become more focused and intense.

Concentration meditation is considered to be the only technique in traditional Tibetan meditation that enables a person to reach the extraordinary state of mind of *shi nay,* by practicing intensely for years and in isolation. Shi nay means something similar to "calm abiding."*

In this state of greatest, undisturbed, and purest concentration, the practicing individual can reach the specific insight of *lhang-thong,* also known as *vipassana.* Someone who has accomplished this state of absolute clarity of the mind is able to discard the veil of ignorance and see things the way they really are. United with his or her *bodhichitta,* the spirit of enlightenment, this person can recognize the final truth of all phenomena and reach the complete stage of enlightenment in an overwhelming and powerful experience and enter Nirvana just as Buddha Shakyamuni did 2,500 years ago.

As you can see, the potential these meditation techniques harbor is extraordinary. Naturally, you cannot have the same expectations when delving into the following exercises, because you are a normal citizen in these fast-paced times. With certainty, however, you will benefit greatly from an increased ability to concentrate, whether you apply these meditations for spiritual or for secular reasons. Furthermore, these exercises will affect you directly and noticeably, providing you with inner calm and serenity. The path itself that leads to the state of shi nay will bring you an experience of the highest order, which could be interpreted as the final goal.

Every human being, no matter what his or her creed, can reach the wonderful state of the shi nay by means of this meditation. Everybody is equipped with the skills that are necessary to bring about the state of calm abiding.

This meditation is particularly helpful for people who suffer from depression, anxiety, or stress. Specifically, people who make their situation worse by constantly pondering over their depression and pain will find an excellent remedy in concentration meditation, which will temporarily turn their minds

---

*Translator's footnote: "calm abiding" is the technical term; a more general term would be "dwelling in peace."

away from thoughts of suffering. Even those of us who endure physical illness can experience relief of pain to some extent. A meditation of this order that has been conducted fervently for at least ten minutes will cause positive effects in any case.

Overview

Apart from the already established preliminary exercises, it is important to carry out the breathing exercise for the ninefold energy purification (page 26) and, if needed, the breathing exercise on page 31. It is up to you what you choose for the object of meditation. You can pick your own body, your mind, or small items, such as a stone or a candle.

It is important that your inner disposition is positive in respect to the object of meditation; however, this object also should be easy to visualize. A story from the old scriptures relates how a yogi kept looking for still another object for his meditations to reach shi nay, but wasn't able to concentrate on any of them. He tried a great number of objects and finally attained the state of shi nay while meditating on the horn of an ox.

Replenish your motivation. Then use your inner eye to look at the object of meditation that you have planted somewhat elevated within your reach in front of you. Direct your mind slowly and purposefully toward the object of meditation and let it rest upon it. When you have done this, try to remain in this state of resting and "single-pointed focus" concentration for thirty seconds.

In the next step, start over again, and each time try to extend your session a little more. Using this kind of purposeful concentration, carefully try to affix your mind to the object of your meditation.

There is a possibility that the mind will display restlessness and become all too happy to wander off when you try affixing it carefully. It may not even allow you to attach it. This, however, is a normal reaction that should not deter or worry you. A wild animal that has been captured will react in much the same way, and it will fight even more when it is being tied up. After a while, it will give up and go along. Using a stick and hitting the animal instead of waiting patiently until it has calmed down would only make it wilder yet.

The mind will react in much the same way. Therefore, if it should wander, do not restrain it forcefully; instead, take a little break. Gently gather your thoughts for a while, then again try to direct your mind and lead it back to the object of meditation. Eventually, you will be able to affix the mind to the object for longer and longer intervals.

The importance of mindfulness and alertness

This calm-abiding meditation is greatly facilitated by two mental faculties: mindfulness and alertness. Mindfulness will help you notice if the mind has begun to wander, and alertness will aid you in gently bringing it back to the task.

> Remember the two mental faculties in
> concentration meditation:
> Mindfulness
> Alertness

With the help of both these mental faculties, you can carry on with the meditation for a longer period of time. If you practice regularly, you will gradually manage to extend the session—at first to ten minutes, then to fifteen or even twenty minutes. Without pushing yourself, you can continually lengthen the duration of this meditation week by week, month by month, and year by year so that maybe one day you will attain the extraordinarily beautiful state of mind of shi nay. Experienced practitioners can remain for hours in this highest form of concentration, while they are completely unaware of anything that is happening around them.

How to deal with lack of focus and with excitement

There also exist obstacles in concentration meditation. The most important are excitement and lack of focus. These obstacles may show themselves after you have been meditating for a certain length of time. The antidotes for these problems are, again, mindfulness and alertness; these can be used to bring the meditation back onto the right track. When you notice your concentration getting dull and the object of meditation losing its sharp outline, you can use mindfulness to bring the image back into focus. Your concentration on the object may have become so intense, on the other hand, that you get excited, which, in turn, can be detrimental for the meditation. In this case, alertness will help you to stabilize your concentration.

Keep in mind the remedies for lack of focus and for excitement in concentration meditation:
Against lack of focus, use mindfulness.
Against excitement, use alertness.

When you start practicing concentration meditation, do so in small doses. Do not become overly ambitious in the beginning by trying to meditate for more than three minutes. This is particularly true for beginners. Listen to your inner voice and allow yourself to interrupt a session when the time has come. Follow the example of the great experienced practitioners in Tibet. They liken meditation to a sumptuous and delicious meal. The quality of a meal and a meditation depend on the art of moderation. If you take too much, you feel unwell and your pleasure is diminished.

Make yourself a table to record your exercises in concentration meditation:

Date	Duration of full session (in minutes)	Duration of meditation, free of distraction (in minutes)	Lack of focus as reason for distraction (mark with an x)	Excitement as reason for distraction (mark with an x)

SEVENTEEN

Breathing Exercise to Induce the Calm State of Mind

YOU ARE WELL ADVISED TO FOLLOW UP the concentration meditation with the exercise for the calm state of mind. This meditation allows your mind to regenerate after practicing a concentration meditation, which takes a lot of energy.

Keep the same position that you had during the concentration meditation, or, depending on your need, lie down, walk, or sit down. Let your mind and thoughts wander freely and observe them as you would pretty white clouds in a clear, blue sky. While contemplating the thoughts in your mind, you are relaxed and loosened up; you can improve this calm state of mind by diaphragmatic breathing with your stomach rising and falling, which is very comforting. You already know this technique from the breathing visualization on page 58. If it is not familiar to you, just breathe naturally but slowly and deeply.

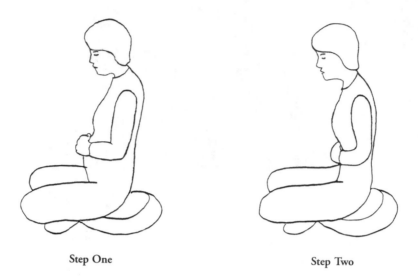

Step One   Step Two

Breathe in slowly and gently through your mouth and feel how your lungs are filling with fresh air. This will provide your tired body with an optimal amount of oxygen. When you *inhale* deeply, notice how your abdominal wall clearly moves out and how the diaphragm moves downward. This movement of up and down massages the organs below in a rhythmical fashion and stimulates them (step one).

Now slowly *exhale* through your slightly opened mouth, from the lungs and the abdomen, purposefully expelling all air. Try to consciously spend more time exhaling than inhaling. Make sure your lungs and the abdomen are completely empty before you furnish them with fresh oxygen (step two).

Concentration meditation combined with the breathing exercise on calming your state of mind will leave you feeling refreshed, relaxed, and calm within a very short period of time. You will sense inner peace and boundless tranquility. You will feel in tune with yourself.

EIGHTEEN

Seven Khum-Lhö Massages for Relaxation

THIS PART OF THE BOOK PRIMARILY ADDRESSES concentration and analytical meditation. Both require utmost concentration, very involved analysis, and deep thinking about the objects of meditation; therefore, I wish to introduce a number of simple massages and exercises to help you to loosen up and relax. In between sessions, self-massages as well as relaxing meditative exercises will improve your disposition and positively affect the course of the meditation.

Fingers

Rest both hands on your knees with the palms of your hands facing up. Use your thumb to press down on your fingers one by one at about the middle joint. Open your hands and spread your fingers wide, then close your hands by putting your thumbs down into your hands and forming a fist, beginning with your pinkie finger. Open your hands, again stretching the fingers wide apart. Repeat this exercise a few times.

Fingers

Hands

Shake your hands up and down, then sideways from right to left, so they can loosen up. Then rub your hands in a slow, washing motion until they feel warm.

Hands

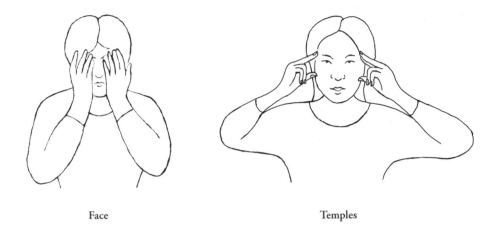

Face   Temples

Face

Stroke your face a few times with your warm hands.

Temples

Point your fingertips up, then bend your pinkie and ring fingers. Bring the middle and index fingers to your temples and rest your thumbs on your cheeks. Massage your temples in a gentle circulating motion.

Eyebrows

Pick up the inner sides of your eyebrows between your thumbs and your index fingers and move your fingers slowly to the other ends of your eyebrows by pulling and stroking gently all along.

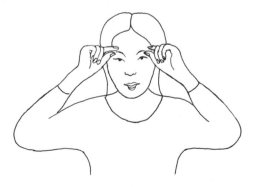

Eyebrows

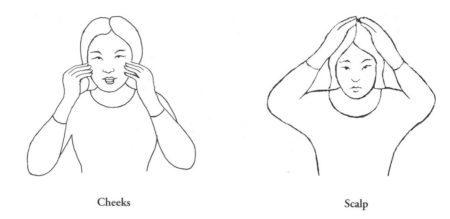

Cheeks   Scalp

Cheeks

Using your fingers and opposing thumb, very gently pull all over on the skin of your cheeks.

Scalp

Put your hands on your head. Spread your fingers over your scalp, massaging it lightly, beginning in the front and moving toward the back.

Shoulders

Place your right hand lightly onto your left shoulder. While pushing gently, let your hand glide over your shoulder toward your chest, then let it rest on your right knee. Now take your left hand and put it lightly onto your right shoulder, pushing down gently, gliding forward, and then resting the hand on your left knee.

Shoulders

Feet

Take one foot at a time and set it at an angle over your other leg. Take your foot into your hands and lightly massage the sole. Loosen your ankle joint as well by rotating your foot a little.

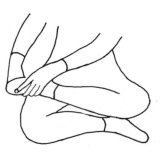

Feet

Seven Meditative Lü-Gom Exercises

THE MEDITATIVE PHYSICAL EXERCISES that follow do not merely focus on physical activity, but also are geared to one's mental disposition while doing the exercise. You have the ability to emphasize the effects of each exercise by doing it with the strong and heartfelt resolve that the exercise will help reinforce your inner positive strength and provide you with a calm and collected state of mind, which is necessary for harmonious cohabitation with others. Each exercise has its own specific descriptive name. Try to meditate about the meaning of this name and let it grow inside of you while you are doing the exercise. The physical activity contributes to loosen and relax tense muscles in your body. It fills you with a sense of external well-being. Mind training combined with external well-being from physical relaxation causes a distinct improvement in your quality of life, shaped by inner strength and tolerance.

Modesty ❖

Take up a relaxed, seated position. Hold your legs in a comfortable position. Rest your hands on your knees. As you inhale, gently straighten out your back, lightly lifting your chest and stretching it forward, while gently pulling back both shoulder blades without applying any force. Stretch your neck a little so that your chin moves forward. Look straight ahead. In this position, your hands automatically will be slightly pulled up on your thighs (step one).

The next time you *exhale,* relax your back, your shoulders, and finally, your head, curling into a loose ball. You are looking down to the ground. Your hands slide back to the original position and rest on your knees (step two).

Repeat this exercise at least three times.

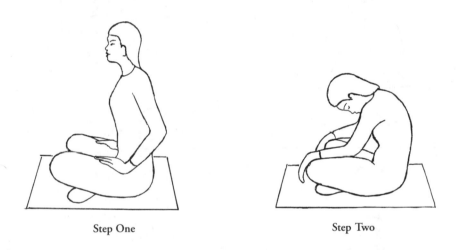

Step One   Step Two

Putting Negative Thoughts to Rest ❖

This exercise can be done while sitting on the floor, on a chair, or even while standing up. Those who have practiced a lot stand with their legs far apart.

Take up your starting position with your hands resting on your knees or on your thighs if you chose the standing position The palms of your hands should be face up while forming a loose fist (step one). When you breathe in, bring both fists up to your ears (step two). Then twist your hands so that the thumbs are next to your cheeks (step three).

Bring both arms gently up to your sides while opening your hands. The palms of your hands should face away from you with your fingers pointing up. While straightening out your back, tense up your arms, including your wrists, for a short moment (step four).

Step One   Step Two

Step Three   Step Four

Step Five

The next time you *exhale,* relax your back, arms, and hands, gently lower your arms and set your hands palm side up on your knees (step five).

Repeat this exercise at least three times.

Wisdom ❖

Stand with your legs slightly apart. People who have had a lot of practice use a wider angle. Form the gesture of wisdom with both your hands by pushing the insides of your thumbs and your ring fingers against each other while holding your remaining fingers straight. Your arms should be slightly bent and lifted in front of you (step one).

Step One

When you *inhale,* bring both hands about forty-five degrees to the right. Your right hand is a little higher than the left one (at about eye level), the palms of your hands face away from you, and your wrists are pushed forward lightly (step two).

Your shoulders remain loose and relaxed. Follow your hands with your eyes. With a movement of your arms to the upper right, straighten out your legs (step three).

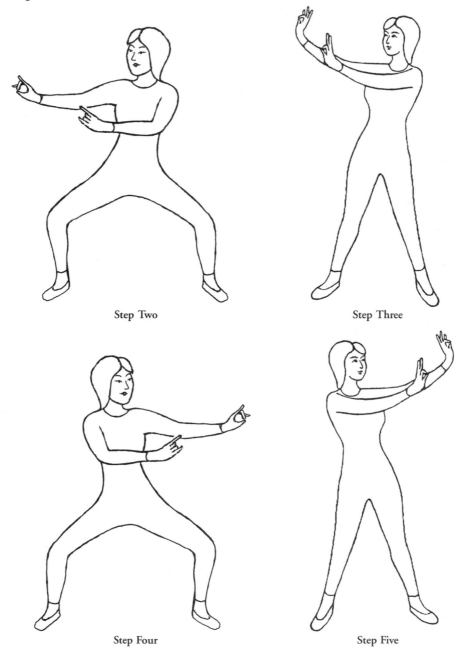

Step Two   Step Three

Step Four   Step Five

When you *exhale,* relax your hands and bring them down in front of your body toward the left with the palms facing up. As your arms are coming down, bend your knees again (step four). When you take the next breath, repeat the same exercise, but moving your hands to your left side (step five).

Repeat the exercise on both sides for at least three times in a row. At the end, open your hands and bring them down to your sides, hanging loosely while you straighten out your legs.

Affection ❖

Your legs should be straight and slightly apart. When you *inhale,* bring your relaxed arms up to shoulder level (step one). Set both hands (arms) down crosswise on your chest, with the right hand on top of the left one. The next time you *exhale,* tilt your upper body slowly to the right and straighten it out again. Keep breathing normally (step two).

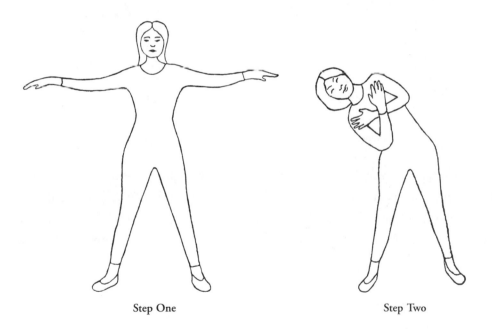

Step One   Step Two

The next time you *inhale,* open your arms as if you were going to embrace someone. Then put your hands back down over your chest crosswise, but this time with your left hand on top.

Repeat this exercise at least three times.

Humility ❖

Stand with your legs apart. As you *inhale,* slowly bring both arms sideways above your head, with your shoulders remaining relaxed (step one).

Step One   Step Two

When you *exhale,* begin bending your straight upper body forward until both arms and body are parallel to the ground. (Keep your legs straight during this time—you will sense light tension in your leg muscles.) Your focus lies ahead of you. Hold this position for a moment, then *exhale* completely. The next time you *inhale,* bring your hands together in a praying gesture with a beautiful opening and closing circular motion (step two).

Gently let your hands, head, and upper body drop down. If necessary, bend your knees a little so it is easy for you to touch the ground with the tips of your fingers. (Experienced practitioners will touch the ground with the palms of their hands during this part of the exercise.) Exhale slowly at this point (step three).

Slowly raise your upper body now, while keeping your knees bent. At the same time, breathe *in.* Leave your arms hanging loosely by your sides. Let your sacrum settle at a lower point for your body to be able to straighten out naturally. During the last phase of rising up, you *exhale* (step four).

Repeat this exercise at least three times.

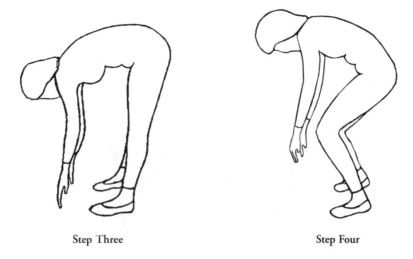

Step Three   Step Four

Tolerance ❖

You should be sitting on the ground; your legs are stretched out next to each other. As you *inhale,* raise your hands up at the sides of your body (step one). Then bring them together in front of your chest in a praying gesture. Your hands are applying some pressure, pushing against each other (step two).

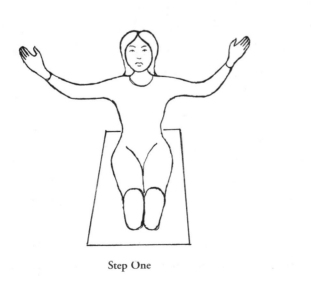
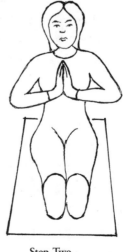

Step One   Step Two

The next time you *exhale,* open your hands, set them down on your thighs and let them slide forward toward your ankles. This automatically will bring your upper body forward as well. Let your head dangle in a relaxed manner (step three).

People who have had a lot of practice can bend forward so much that they are able to lightly pull back on their toes with their fingers or, with legs apart, they can slide their palms forward between their legs (step four).

Step Three

Step Four

Peace of Mind ❖

In a relaxed fashion, lie down on the ground, with your arms at your sides and the palms of your hands facing down (step one). As you breathe in, put both hands on your thighs and slowly try to lift your upper body a little. This will be easier if you tighten your abdominal muscles (step two).

The next time you breathe out, let your upper body sink back down to the ground (step three).

Repeat this part three times.

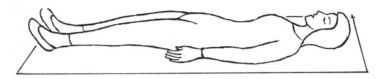

Step One

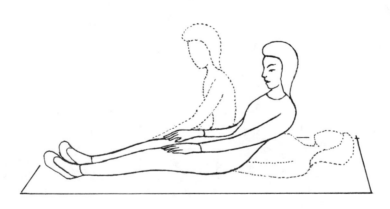

Steps Two and Three

After the third repetition, put your hands on your belly so you will be able to feel your breathing. For at least three times, inhale and exhale deeply. Every time you *exhale* try to sense the whole length of your back touching the ground. Imagine that every breath you take reinforces your inner strength and that this power grants you immense peace. Remain in this state of peace of mind and let it settle inside of you (step four).

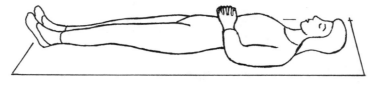

Step Four

TWENTY

Analytical Meditation

YOU HAVE LEARNED IN THE CHAPTER ON concentration meditation that many reasons for suffering can be found within ourselves; they are part of the nature of our minds. However, what are the reasons for all suffering, and what would we like to explore? Analytical meditation thoroughly examines these questions and is a type of Tibetan Buddhist meditation described as "flowing" or "flexible." Different from concentration meditation, in which the mind is pointedly tied to the object and is sort of immobile, the analytical task is to investigate actively, paying attention to every little detail by pondering deeply upon the true nature of the object. We explore the object of meditation by taking it apart into different components.

Before introducing the different methods, I would like to explain the Tibetan Buddhist meaning of transgression and, specifically, how we interpret the term "ignorance."

The meaning of ignorance

In studying the nature and function of the mind, we have discovered that the mind is seriously blinded by the effects of three delusions: greed, hate, and ignorance. Therefore, it is responsible for all wrongful actions. The Tibetans have called these transgressions the three poisons of the mind and, of the three, ignorance is thought to be at the root of all that is evil. It is due to ignorance that greed develops—a form of exaggerated attachment and obsessive desire—which, in turn, will produce hate toward everything that blocks the way of the desire, keeping it from being fulfilled.

Ignorance lets us believe, and even be perfectly convinced, in the true existence of the "I"-ness.*

Because we are convinced that the I-ness does exist, we are very attached to our body because we believe the body to be the I-ness. We will react with hate and aggression to anybody intending to harm our body. Even to death, we will defend all our possessions, our family, or our country in the same manner, because we are tied to them in body and spirit.

You may think that this is only natural that we want to do so. This is true. We can observe the animals and notice how they spend all their lives to care for their pack and even defend their territory with their lives. This potentially self-destructive pattern of behavior can be observed among all living creatures.

We, however, differ from animals in that we have the ability to study and explore this pattern that causes suffering and possibly find an answer that in the future will keep us from being dependent on the selfishness that brings about the three poisons of our mind.

Tibetan meditation teaches us that the root cause of all suffering is to be found in the negative disposition of the mind called ignorance. This ignorance (*ma-rigpa* in Tibetan) means not seeing things the way they really are. It keeps us from recognizing the final truth called *dag-me,* the nonexistence of the I-ness. Thus, Tibetan philosophy teaches the nonexistence of the I-ness. People are asked not to passively accept this fact; instead, they are urged to inquire

---

*Translator's footnote: The awkward but self-explanatory term "I-ness," literally translated from the German original "Ich-heit" (also very unusual in German), depicts the difficulty in defining a context that deals with specific terms in a variety of subjects. Others have used the terms "ego" or "self" in their translations of the same context of Tibetan Buddhism, whose equivalents in German the author avoided.

carefully, checking and analyzing its premise for its steadfastness. We use analytical meditation to carry out this task; it is not dependent on any belief system and therefore anyone can practice it, regardless of creed.

Before we go looking for this I-ness, we will have to be able to identify it and get to know its characteristics. It is like looking for Mrs. Smith, knowing neither her address nor what she may look like. Therefore, you need to get information before you set out to look for her, for example, where she lives and her characteristics.

We start our search for the I-ness with the same question: Where does it reside? When I ask my students the question about the home of the I-ness, they all point to their own body, which is only natural, of course. To us, the body is equivalent to the I-ness. In Tibetan Buddhist view, the body as a whole is composed of five different aggregates (*skandhas* in Sanskrit). In this concept, the entire human being consists of the following:

- The aggregate of the form
- The aggregate of emotions or sensations
- The aggregate of recognition or perception
- The aggregate of conceptual formation or intellect
- The aggregate of consciousness

The *aggregate of the form* shapes the body purely in its material form, that is, bones, skin, hair, organs, brain, blood, nerves, etc.

The *aggregate of emotions or sensations* relates to the perception of hot or cold, pain, happiness, and all sort of other feelings, whether they are positive, negative, or neutral.

The *aggregate of recognition or perception* is used for noticing the shape or form of things. Look at any item that may be right in front of you now, for example, a pencil. You can see that it is long, round, pointed at one end, and green. Thus, you recognize its pure form.

With the *aggregate of conceptual formation or intellect,* not only do you see the pure form of the item but you also know its function. Of the pencil, you know that you can write with it. Here we are talking about the activity of the mind that brings function to the form.

The *aggregate of consciousness* is the most important of all aggregates and has an influence on all of the others. The consciousness of your senses—seeing, hearing, smelling, tasting—and that of your body are part of this component, as are the three poisons of hate, greed, and ignorance.

The last four aggregates are tied in with the mind. This shows that the Buddhists believe that the mind has much more meaning than merely being responsible for thinking and/or intellect. The mind is not only located in the head, but is found everywhere in the body. It is the mind that is responsible for bringing life to the material body. Buddhist philosophy is very involved in studying this aspect, but if you try to make sense of just the basic concept, you will clearly understand that all parts that make up a human being are of a passing nature. They are all subject to change.

When we start out looking for the I-ness, we will ask for the whereabouts of the I-ness. Is it located in the mind or in the body? It does not make sense to point to our body and insist that it be our "I."

> When Tibetan Buddhists talk about the nonexistence of the I-ness, do not misunderstand and believe that it means that we do not even exist in reality. This would take the idea too far, because everybody is aware of his or her existence. We are really present; otherwise, it would be impossible to explain our being.

In practicing analytical meditation, you will discover and understand that the I-ness does not exist in rigid or unchangeable form, as you may have assumed until now. The I-ness is not an entity that carries on, isolated and independent of everything else that exists, but it is a phenomenon that is supported by the five aggregates. Our mind, being blinded by ignorance, conceives I-ness on the basis of the five aggregates and causes us to be tangled up in patterns of behavior that are full of mistakes and that lead to suffering.

You can apply the following analysis to all existing phenomena. You then will come to the conclusion that no single phenomenon is independent of other phenomena. The phenomenon does not exist all by itself.

We are ignorant as long as we look upon phenomena and ourselves as entities of their own that exist independently of other phenomena.

It is not easy to grasp this aspect of the nonexistence of the I-ness or the emptiness of the phenomena. It takes many years of practice in analytical meditation to achieve absolute realization, which means seeing things as they really are. These teachings make up an important part of higher mind training in Tibetan philosophy.

People currently live in hectic times and are constantly searching for explanations for their suffering and the means to relieve it. Analytical meditation offers us assistance, despite the fact that we may not yet have come to the absolute realization or found an insight in I-lessness. Our rigid concept of the solid and unchangeable I-ness is questioned and exposed; suddenly our attitude changes toward ourselves and toward others, and we are able to make a positive change in our lives now. Not only will you be able to recognize your own rigid behavioral patterns, but you will also be more able to easily do something about them. In addition, you will recognize changes within yourself as well as in other people around you. It becomes impossible to form an inflexible opinion about another person—either in a positive or negative sense.

Tibetan Buddhism has numerous different types of analytical meditations that address this context. I wish to introduce you to four of these, which are particularly effective:

- The meditation on emptiness of phenomena
- The meditation on the impermanence of phenomena
- The meditation on patience and tolerance
- The meditation on love and compassion

The Meditation on Emptiness of Phenomena

❖ ❖ ❖

RECOGNIZING THE EMPTINESS OF ALL PHENOMENA is the key to understanding the ultimate truth. This meditation will help you above all to battle ignorance. In doing the following analytical meditation, you will have the opportunity to thoroughly get to know the "I" as well as learn to identify it.

After you have brought about the calm state of mind and you are beautifully relaxed from doing the physical exercises, you can start this meditation on emptiness.

Using your mind's eye, visualize a strip of rainbow color, similar to the "I" image on page 127. If you would like to use the illustration of the "I or the "rainbow body" as your object of meditation for the following exercises, you can post them on the wall, a little elevated from the ground. It is important that you are able to look down on the object while comfortably sitting in your customary position for meditation.

Enter the answers that you discover during the second and third kinds of analysis in the following table.

Meditation date	Form of analysis	Where the "I" is located

MANJUSHRI MANTRA (CD TRACK 18)

During each kind of analysis, it is recommended to listen to the mantra of Manjushri, the deity of wisdom.

Om ara patsa na di di di di di di di . . .

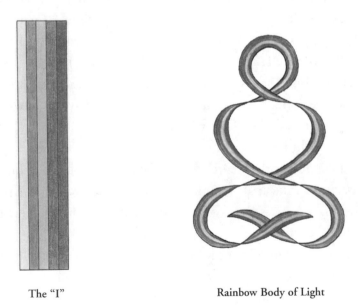

The "I"   Rainbow Body of Light

The First Type of Analysis ❖❖❖

Very calmly, set out to study the "I." What is its shape, what is its size, what are its colors? You clearly can see that it consists of five parts, each a different color. In your imagination, you can peel off the blue stripe and ask yourself, Which is the part that embodies the "I" now? Is it in the four remaining parts or is it in the blue stripe? Are there possibly two "I"s now? Where is it now, the "I"?

One after the other, peel off the other stripes of color and each time ask yourself the relevant questions.

The Second Type of Analysis ❖❖❖

In this meditation, you apply the first type of analysis to yourself.

You can look upon the illustrations of the rainbow body or the letter "I" on page 127 as symbols of your own body, which is held together by the five aggregates. Now start searching for the "I." Where is it located?

If you believe your "I" is located exclusively in your body, write down in which part of your body it is to be found. If you believe your "I" is located in your mind, write down which phase of the mind that is. ("Phase" in this sense is a developmental phase of your mind. Since childhood your mind has been steadily changing, like a river that never remains the same on its journey from the spring to the delta where it meets the ocean.) Thus, where is the "I" located—the one that is important enough to cause you to be egocentric at times? Where actually can you find the "I" that drives you to be greedy, that you must have everything for yourself?

Where is it hiding?

Now take on another search for the I-ness in the form of an alert and careful inspection. Take apart your body like a puzzle and put each piece down on the ground. Where is the "I" located? Is it in your head, your trunk, in your legs, or in your arms?

Separate your body into the aggregates form and mind. Take the aggregate of the form apart further into smaller and smaller material parts, even to the point of billions of tiny atoms. The parts get so small that they finally cease to exist, and with them disappears the I-ness.

In the next step, take a look at the mind. It is composed of beautiful and sad memories from early childhood and youth, and memories of the present as well as the future. Separate these parts as you did before. The components here become smaller and smaller again until they cease to exist. As these parts disappear, so does the I-ness.

Become aware that your rigid concept of a solid and completely independent "I" is very faulty. A mind blinded by ignorance caused you to project body and mind held together by the five aggregates as an independent, indestructible existence. Because of this perceived existence of I-ness, people have developed all sorts of desires and attachments. You have confronted with resentment everybody and everything that have threatened your objects of desire. Blinded by the negative state of mind—that is, ignorance—your ability to see the ultimate truth of all phenomena is obstructed.

Because of the nonexistence of the I-ness, there is no need for desire and attachment. This is a singular and valuable recognition. Subsequently, there is no reason for emotions such as hate or grudges in defending them; your life therefore becomes much more relaxed and comforting. This, in turn, will create the perception of additional space, giving you a sense of more freedom.

According to Buddhist interpretation, the mind that is blinded by ignorance is responsible for our extreme dependence on the "I." The concept of the "I" fosters the terms "my" and "our," which, in turn, will lead to the idea of "the others." This is the origin of the cycle that keeps all of us bound until we set out—pushed by our own ambition and intellect as well as our ability to use analytical meditation—to get to the bottom of all dissatisfaction and unhappiness that afflicts us.

The Third Type of Analysis ❖❖❖

After you thoroughly have explored your own "I," you can start looking for the I-ness of others. To find out what it is that you hate, you will set out to study the I-ness of that particular fellow human whom you dislike the most at the moment, the one who provokes the most negative emotions. This fellow human also is composed of the five aggregates that make up body and mind. Should you be looking for the I-ness of this unloved person in his or her body? If your answer is yes, which part of his or her body contains that

I-ness? Would it possibly be in his or her mind, and which phase of it would that be? Thus, where do you locate that I-ness of the person who causes you so much grief, hate, and loathing? In case you are planning to harm this person, do you wish to cause harm to his or her body or mind?

If there is a certain group of people that triggers an aversion in you, ask yourself the same questions. What specifically is it that you hate about them? Separate the people in this group and look at them one by one. Now ask yourself where exactly has the object of my hate gone to? You will discover that the group you identified does not quite exist anymore, and therefore the targeted object has become insignificant.

This approach to meditation is of particular importance during wars, times of terrorism, discrimination, and other discords that involve groups of people.

The Fourth Type of Analysis ❖ ❖ ❖

Now you can apply this kind of analysis toward objects that affect you with great desire or aversion. With careful and thorough study, try to find out what in particular you find so desirable or deplorable.

Keeping in mind that phenomena do not exist on their own but consist of a number of parts, you will realize quickly how the target of your desire or dislike loses significance.

TWENTY-TWO

Impermanence of Phenomena

❖ ❖ ❖

IN TIBETAN TRADITION, the meditation on the impermanence of phenomena is practiced exclusively for the purpose of remembering one's own mortality and to create a strong aspiration to avoid the development of any type of material desire. Specifically, regular meditation on one's own impermanence is considered a powerful remedy in Tibetan tradition when it comes to the task of regaining a proper perspective in life. A person practicing meditation will recognize how extraordinarily short his or her life really is, which, in turn, will serve as a great incentive to steer clear of squandering that precious time on actions without virtue. Normal people living in a modern society who have made certain sacrifices use this meditation to help them find their way in this secular life. In these times of great unrest and constant change of values, it helps us to stabilize and regain our perspective in life.

Many of us are convinced that life would be easier to deal with by denying the notion of impermanence. The widespread idea that man has ample time at his or her disposal leads to frivolous behavior and superficiality. Many issues are swept under the rug, and many other concerns go by unnoticed. This may apply to things in life that are unpleasant or pleasant.

However, when you become familiar with the impermanence of phenomena, you most certainly will experience life much more intensively, because you will recognize the fact that you have only a fixed amount of time.

What you can do is to look back over the past ten years and calculate the maximum amount of years that you still may be alive. Wouldn't it be a pity then if you couldn't enjoy every single day that is left of your life? But how many days do we spend our time complaining about little things or are unhappy or depressed because something or another did not turn out the way we expected? Even people in good health will constantly find reasons for being dissatisfied.

Then again, nobody can be absolutely sure about being alive tomorrow. It is true that we are living in a world that is highly technical and modern, and practically speaking, anything is possible; still, one cannot purchase a guarantee on the duration of our life. Families have come apart, and their relations are the worst possible. In all their antagonism, not one of the individuals will ponder upon the possibility of one of the other members dying suddenly, without leaving time for reconciliation or spending some wonderful time together. Other people waste their short life spans thinking about material well-being; they are only interested in accumulating more worldly riches and in becoming more powerful. In the meantime, they tend to forget that their time to live is limited; they miss out on enjoying the company of the people around them.

> By regularly practicing the meditation on the impermanence of phenomena, you will become aware of weak spots in your lifestyle. You will have an opportunity to intervene and bring about positive changes.

This meditation is also very helpful if you wish to counter a steady onslaught of desires and attachments. You most certainly have experienced at some time or another how your mind reacts restlessly, nervously, and even aggressively when you desire something that you cannot call your own. And your mind will react in the same manner at times when your ambitions are unrealistic and cannot be fulfilled.

Such thoughts are likely to spoil your entire day, and your inability to shake these ideas makes your mind spin. This kind of dissatisfaction will cause a bad temper, and you are likely to vent your frustration on family members, colleagues, or friends.

By deeply pondering upon the impermanence of phenomena through analytic meditation, you can gain an insight into the short duration and instability of life. For example, you may recognize that your aim was set too high; the object you desired will lose its troubling importance.

The meditation on the impermanence of phenomena further teaches us that all phenomena, whether living creatures or pure matter, have no independent existence of their own, but consist of many parts that make up the whole. According to Tibetan understanding, everything that is assembled from many parts is constantly moving, changing, and never remains the same for a moment. Thus, the law of the impermanence of phenomena governs life itself.

The recognition that phenomena have no lasting existence, but instead are moving and changing constantly, makes it obvious that we will not be able to hold on to all those things that we desire so much or to those people we cling to so passionately. Because of their steady movement and unending transformation, their properties change every moment; thus, they are already no longer the same objects we envisioned earlier. Neither are they the same things that we desired in the beginning. There remains nothing that you can grasp, cling to, or desire. From that follows that nothing exists that you can hold on to with hatred. Think of a beautiful and fragrant bouquet of flowers that you bought with great joy and desire at a farmers' market. In only a few days the flowers will be past their prime and the leaves will have dried up. There is nothing left to remind you of the once beautiful flowers. Even the water in the vase is discolored and smells foul. This example illustrates the impermanence of phenomena; it doesn't imply, however, that we should not allow ourselves such joyful pleasures. With the flowers, we are prepared for the impermanence of their beauty, which, in turn, will make us more appreciative, cause us to look at the flowers more consciously, and increase our feeling of happiness in their presence.

Of all the things that are changing constantly, we need to look to our mind in particular. One moment you believe your mind is with you, but an instant later, you notice that your mind is with somebody else you know or it is in a faraway country visiting one of your aunts. Not much later and your mind is back again, feeling happy. Depending on the subject at hand, your mind then may become unhappy. The next thing you know it has recovered and appears to be completely excited about something, only to be angry in another moment, perhaps starting to complain. You fall in love, and you spend all your time thinking about that one person. Suddenly, you wish to never see that person again and may even develop hatred toward that person.

All of us are very familiar with these phases of change. You can look inside yourself to confirm this. Doesn't your mind seem like a gigantic train station with trains coming and going at a steady pace, rushing, and with people hopping on trains that depart to all different directions? Comparably, our thought processes, emotions, and perceptions are racing this way and that, each speeding on to different destinations and changing course without interruption. The following exercise will help you to bring peace to that commotion.

Because it is not easy to imagine one's personal impermanence, I recommend that you start out meditating upon a simple process of impermanence. This process is well known and easy to visualize, and it is a subject that, emotionally, will only touch you a little.

The first step of this exercise is to visualize the impermanence of a flower; in the next step, you apply the concept to yourself.

How to do the exercise

Following the customary preparations, carefully check your posture and begin the meditation on the impermanence of phenomena.

FIRST STEP
I recommend that you take a beautiful fresh flower for your meditation object and place it in a vase that stands within reach on the floor or is somewhat elevated. As an alternative, you have the option of visualizing the flower with your imaginary eye.

Now think of the development of this beautiful flower. Carefully recall the process of how it started out as a seed that was put in the ground; the little seed sprouts and grows roots that take deep hold in the earth. The seedling then breaks the surface of the ground, and every day it stretches higher toward the sun. The plant gets bigger and stronger and sprouts tender green leaves and buds. From those buds then spring colorful fragrant blossoms; it brings you joy just to look at them. The plant reaches its peak of beauty and radiance.

All other phenomena are equally subject to the law of impermanence of all things, as is this flower. The plant, regardless of how beautiful it is or how delightful the splendors its of blossoms, is like a small natural wonder. In time, the leaves and blossoms lose their shine and fall to the ground. Using its remaining energy, the flower brings out the seeds for the next generation and wilts away. What is left is the stem without leaves that eventually will rot and recombine with the earth.

Second step

Consciously look upon the normal course of a human life. Integrate your personal experience in this meditation.

We start our journey toward old age at the moment we are born; the first breath we take and every breath thereafter brings us closer to our death. We have grown older with every breath that accompanied us since childhood.

In the beginning, you may find it difficult to accept this because you have only rarely or never thought about your own impermanence. Consider a life span of about eighty years and deduct the first ten years of childhood and the last thirty years of old age; you are left with forty years, half of which you spend sleeping. Thus, you have twenty years of peak physical and mental capacity. Wouldn't it be a pity if you could not spend those short precious years consciously aware and in harmony with yourself and the people around you? Is it worth spending that precious time being driven by the three poisons and hatefully fighting your enemies, or on increasing your property because you are driven by desires, or by changing your friends along the way?

When you were young, time seemed endless to you, because you were striving to be like a grown-up. When you become a grown-up, you get caught up in your activities, you start a family, bring up your kids, and can hardly wait for them to be done with their education.

During all this time, you have aged tremendously; your children have grown up now and are starting their own families. They bring home their little ones, your grandchildren, who will call you grandma and grandpa. Despite the fact that grandparents nowadays like to act young and try to look that way as long as possible, there is no denying that the inner biological clock keeps ticking. Problems of old age keep mounting and, just like that beautiful flower, you lose your youthful appearance. Your strength weakens. When the first dear friends of your own age start passing away, you start mentally preparing yourself and hope for a quiet and dignified death. After you die, your lifeless body will be put into a coffin and be burned or buried. Nothing will remain of the body that you were so attached to your entire life.

Important considerations

It is not the goal of this meditation on impermanence that you become indifferent in life, that you lose control of yourself, or that you don't enjoy things anymore because everything is only temporary. When applied correctly, the knowledge of the nature of impermanence becomes a strong motivator for you to resolve to thankfully enjoy every moment of your life; this is based on implementing virtues in leading your life. If you experience a depressive or similar emotion while doing this exercise, you need to end the session. Instead, do this exercise at another time when you are well centered and feel more stable.

As soon as you think about death, many things will gain a new perspective, and you may find satisfaction with fewer material things. Instead, you will then strive for more spiritual riches. It is possible that this will improve your personal happiness. Your family, on the other hand, might become dismayed and express their belief that you have the potential for much higher goals in life. In this context, it is important not to confuse your satisfaction and sense of relaxation with laziness. In the spiritual world, monks do not grow lethargic and lazy because of meditation; instead, they aspire to an even more elevated level of mind training. In the same manner, meditation is meant to help you improve your quality of life in the secular world, not in a material sense, but in respect to strengthening your inner qualities. Meditation becomes a steady companion, which positively influences your life and the lives of people around you.

TWENTY-THREE

The Meditation on Patience and Tolerance

❖ ❖ ❖

THE MEDITATION ON PATIENCE AND TOLERANCE will assist you in many aspects of everyday life in becoming aware of the influence of the three poisons, or delusions, of the mind: hate, greed, and ignorance. Patience and tolerance, are the most important antidotes in dealing with those three poisons. Patience means controlling the mind, and tolerance is the understanding of the negative attributes of your fellow humans.

We, however, are not born with the concepts of patience and tolerance, nor do they develop on their own over the years. Frequently, it takes years of practice and experience to master these virtues perfectly. Partial success with mastering these virtues is possible at an early stage, and this will motivate you to proceed with this exercise. You soon will recognize how much better you feel with this new kind of behavior when you react to somebody else, and you will notice a change in the behavior of other people you interact with. The meditation of patience and tolerance enables you to better control spontaneous actions and speech, and avoid negative consequences. In the future, for example, you will be able to turn around a situation in which you feel unfairly criticized and look at it as an opportunity to learn and practice patience and tolerance. Most of all, you will be able to avoid those reactions that caused you to be unhappy, or that possibly made you feel guilty because you hurt somebody else.

You can also use this method spontaneously, in the form of a brief meditation (see page 140). When somebody is hurting you, for instance, you may feel like taking revenge. As soon as you become adept at short meditations, you will recognize quickly that such a reaction will cause negative consequences; you will rescue the situation in that decisive moment and react accordingly in a wiser and more intelligent way. A short meditation is also particularly beneficial at those times when you have to make an important decision.

Many conflicts among people could be solved more peacefully and intelligently if a greater number of people would practice this meditation on a regular basis. On a highest level, politicians could avoid great conflicts and wars with these analytical means.

How to do the exercise

Do the preliminary practices for the meditation and renew your motivation; then begin the meditation on patience and tolerance. Your object of meditation can be any everyday life situation with friends, children, or colleagues in which you sensed your own impatience or intolerance. Let the situation pass before your eyes like the rerun of a movie.

For you to better understand the process, here follows an example of how you can go about that procedure:

> Mrs. Angry and Mrs. Aggressive are caught up in a serious argument. Suddenly, Mrs. Angry insults Mrs. Aggressive by saying, "You stupid cow!" This statement sets off a bout of outraged fury in Mrs. Aggressive. She reacts by becoming verbally abusive, and her reaction culminates in slapping Mrs. Anger in the face. This, in turn, causes Mrs. Angry to feel guilty because she knows that it was her reaction in the beginning that caused the problem.

Because she was upset, Mrs. Angry insulted Mrs. Aggressive by calling her a stupid cow. Now you can analyze the word "cow," which caused Mrs. Aggressive to become so upset. What is the meaning of the word *cow?* In general, there is nothing negative about that term. There is absolutely no sharp edge associated with it that could have hurt Mrs. Aggressive. It is the mind of Mrs. Aggressive that views the term *cow* as negative because of thought patterns that are well entrenched. Mrs. Aggressive's mind, being blinded by ignorance, projects the word *cow* in the context of something deeply insulting. Her mind's "assistants," language and body, reacted accordingly.

Now concentrate your analysis on Mrs. Angry, the one who spoke those words. It is true that she said those words, but she did so because her mind was obscured by ignorance. It was merely the "assistant" language that carried out the action. Who should be blamed in this case—the "assistant" or the unpredictable and tricky mind?

Pretend you are Mrs. Aggressive now; you were just being insulted with "you stupid cow," while being threatened by wild gestures.

Observe your own reactions. Are you able to let such verbal abuse roll off your shoulders or will you be driven to raging anger and slap Mrs. Angry in the face?

A practiced mind will demonstrate patience and tolerance at this moment and let the outrage pass over his or her meditating head. In the eyes of the other person, such behavior may at first be labeled as a weak personality trait, or it may indicate a degree of loss of face; still, in Buddhist terms, that person who acted without aggression is the real winner. This is the moment he or she has conquered his or her worst enemies—the three poisons that are in the nature of the mind. This person successfully avoided being driven to a hostile reaction.*

Now think about the consequences of a counterattack. It is true that you have the ability to hurt the person who is attacking you, and possibly that will give you personal satisfaction. Still, the aggressor will be further encouraged in his or her hatred toward you. At the next opportunity, the aggressor may be more determined in his or her attempt to cause you harm in return. You would not have one minute of peace, because you would have to be prepared for the counterattack. The basis for peaceful coexistence has been disturbed.

There still will be many instances in which you will find it too difficult to tame your anger. This would be a situation in which you make use of the brief meditation on patience and tolerance. Together with the breathing exercise for

---

*Translator's footnote: The German proverb "Der Klügere gibt nach," literally, "the more intelligent person will know to give way" was used in the original text but has no equivalent.

harmonizing body and soul (page 31), this brief meditation will help you to master those kinds of difficult situations. The breathing exercise will help you to reduce your anger on a physical level, and the analytical meditation on patience and tolerance guides you in defeating the three poisons of mind—and allows your anger to dissipate.

Important considerations

This analytical meditation on patience and tolerance is different from other meditations in one important way: You are not provided with exact guidelines; you meditate independently upon a certain course of action.

There is, however, one general guideline that you can follow:

Start by analyzing your "opponent." Try to recognize that his or her mind is the culprit, and that it is further responsible for any of your opponent's actions. Study the mind's assistants, speech and body. Be aware that the mind operates under the strong influence of the three poisons. All this will make it easier for you to practice tolerance.

A Brief Meditation on Patience and Tolerance

At the times when you would like to display patience and tolerance, ask yourself in each situation about the outcome of your reaction in terms of the effect it has on others. Immediately before taking action, pause for a moment and put yourself in the other person's shoes. By taking the path of premeditating an outcome and sensing how painfully someone else will experience your actions or words, you can change your course of action. In this manner, you have the opportunity to contribute immensely to avoid a great deal of suffering and other problems. This type of brief meditation furthermore can be very effective in terms of a positive outcome at times when you have to make important decisions.

In the next step, analyze yourself: Do I have the ability to take such verbal and physical onslaught? What is my advantage if I decide to give way? If I behave like a "pacifist," will there be peace for me and the other person? Will I lose face in the process? Would that be a problem here?

What disadvantage would I have to face should I decide on a counterattack? I possibly could defeat my opponent. The disadvantage here would be as follows: A violent attitude breeds still more violence. The result would be perpetual conflict, and we would no longer be able to live in peace.

This type of meditation is particularly interesting and insightful; however, there is the problem that the mind might decide to wander from the subject at hand or beyond the framework of the meditation.

I like to compare this kind of meditation with watching a criminal scene in a movie: Intending to solve the case, I will have to carefully pay attention to all actions up to the very end. A brief distraction can cause me to fail to reconstruct the entire context.

It is exactly the same with this meditation. Here you also have to think hard to hold your concentration until the very end. You make use of the two mental faculties, mindfulness and alertness, as shown in the section on concentration meditation. Should your mindfulness indicate that your mind has left the framework of the meditation, you can take the faculty of alertness to gently and carefully guide it back to the subject at hand.

You can take advantage of this method in everyday life by meditating upon situations of conflict and confrontation. For you to be successful in your endeavor, it is utterly important that you are motivated by the desire to have the strength to apply what you have learned in your everyday life when the situations arise. Therein lie the essence and the art of Tibetan meditation.

TWENTY-FOUR

The Meditation on Love and Compassion

❖ ❖ ❖

WHEN I SPEAK OF LOVE AS PART of the meditation on love and compassion, I think of love in a universal sense. This love includes all living creatures, whether they are friends, enemies, or neutral.

> Someone who is driven by the wish for all creatures to be free from suffering is showing compassion.
> Someone who is driven by the wish for all creatures to experience happiness is showing love.

Generally, we tend to categorize the people around us into three groups. The first and most important group is that of our family and close friends, those who mean us well. We have very positive feelings toward the people in this category. The second group of people are our enemies, those who do not wish us well. We have a great aversion toward these people. The third group includes neutral people, those who don't have either positive or negative sentiments toward us. We sense indifferent neutrality in respect to these people.

Because we have practiced concentration and analytic meditation, we have learned that our past emotions of greed and desire, our attachments, as well as hatred and anger are without a tangible base. Therefore, we should not categorize other people as friends or foes. This valuable insight is a prerequisite for us to be able to successfully meditate on love and compassion.

> Always remind yourself that your tendency to label the people around you as friends, enemies, and neutral did not develop by itself. You have been influenced by outside circumstances. These influences and circumstances are constantly subject to change. Therefore, one friend today may be your enemy tomorrow. The person who is neutral today may turn out to be your significant other in the near future. Even more important, a person you hate very much at this moment may suddenly turn out to be your best friend.

Before transforming your feelings of hatred into feelings of love, you first need to neutralize your emotions—the way you wash a dirty garment before drying it.

Practice equanimity in your endeavor to neutralize your sentiments of greed and hate. The following example explains the term "equanimity": Imagine you have the ability to assume three body positions at the same time. Leaning over to the extreme right signifies intense greed and attachment toward your friends; leaning over to the extreme left signifies burning hatred toward your enemies; and the middle position, relaxed and straight, represents the composure you demonstrate toward neutral people. The middle position of equanimity is the only one to take up in your quest to develop universal love and universal compassion.

Now try to transfer this example onto a psychological level. Who are the people that trigger in you emotions of extreme attachment or aversion? Who are the people that cause you to be neutral? Be aware that not clinging to somebody does not mean that you should avoid showing affection. Children, for instance, will instinctively shy away and defend themselves from people who demonstrate clutching affection, because they sense that they are being hampered in their free development. Do not mistake this statement as a direction not to show love and affection toward your children; it merely is a warning to avoid clinging to a child.

When you have attained a state of equanimity, you can begin with the meditation on love and compassion. You will open your heart now and show more affection and compassion toward people in your close vicinity—and also toward yourself. You can certainly also pick your own visualizations when doing the following meditation.

How to do the meditation

Do all your preliminary preparations and start the meditation. With great enthusiasm, imagine that you have gathered all the suffering creatures on earth in one country, where, with great expectation, they hope that their suffering will be relieved. Empowered by your endless universal love and compassion, you are bathing the entire land in warm rays of light that affect all living creatures gathered here. These warm and comforting rays of light penetrate the creatures affected by suffering and permeate them with happiness and contentment.

With deep compassion and pure love, visualize enormous rain clouds that come over a land where people and animals are dying because of a severe drought and let the rain come down on the land, the people, and the animals, saving everything and providing them with enough water to live on.

CHENREZI MANTRA (CD TRACK 17)
Recite the Chenrezi mantra of boundless compassion.

Om mani padme hum.

TWENTY-FIVE

The Meditation on Giving and Taking: Tonglen

❖ ❖ ❖

A MEDITATION PRACTICED FREQUENTLY among the Tibetans is called the Tonglen practice of giving and taking. This meditation is very special because the person who is practicing it takes it upon him- or herself to spread his or her healthy energy to all suffering living creatures with an intense feeling of love and compassion. You can intensify the effect of this meditation with the help of the breathing technique that is described on page 31.

What is most important in this method of meditation is your heartfelt motivation to help all living creatures by taking upon yourself all their suffering. Obviously, this will not cause you to be overwhelmed by pain and suffering. Neither will you experience the pain the other creatures are suffering. The important point here is that you are willing to take their suffering upon yourself, and that you are able to do so while creating a feeling of deep and honest love and compassion.

How to do the exercise

While visualizing the following, carry out the breathing technique on the harmonization of body and soul on page 31.

- *Inhale* and take in the suffering of all creatures in the form of dark rays.
- *Exhale* and visualize how you distribute your positive energy in the form of pure, white rays of light to these creatures, which will hereafter allow them to live free from pain and suffering and full of contented happiness.

Tonglen has an important function in people who are suffering from a serious illness. Tibetans believe that this meditation will give meaning to the suffering. The sick person already has to suffer and therefore he or she can carry the suffering of others. With the support of deep love and compassion, the motivation arises that one can bear the suffering of all living creatures in addition to one's own. According to Tibetan Buddhism, the suffering of others will be eased by taking up this burden. Thus, the personal pain of the sick person who meditates is seen in a different perspective. The idea that you bear your own pain for the well-being of all other creatures gives new meaning to your illness and the possibly hopeless condition, transforming it into a meaningful and healing situation.

CHENREZI MANTRA (CD TRACK 17)
Recite the Chenrezi mantra to intensify the effect of this meditation.

Om mani padme hum.

Important considerations

In practicing this meditation on giving and taking, there have been many students who find it difficult to imagine taking in the suffering of all living creatures. They are afraid that this will cause them to become sicker then they are already. This fear is intensified in the visualization in which the personal healthy energy is given to other suffering living beings. Even though such fears are unfounded, you should wait and do the exercise at a later point if you sense this kind of hesitation within yourself. I also recommend expelling those dark rays of suffering from the body by exhaling vigorously at the end of the exercise and to let those rays dissipate in the air.

At this point, I would like to remind you that it is a goal of Tibetan meditation to support and improve human inner development. Just as we keep taking classes or workshops to increase our knowledge within our professions in order to excel, our minds need stimulation of the kind that advances our inner world. The meditation on giving and taking primarily is set up to serve these goals and cannot cause any harm. On the contrary, this exercise, as part of the school of higher mind training in Tibetan meditation, will turn out to be of the greatest advantage to you when you practice it wholeheartedly.

TWENTY-SIX
Closing Remarks

IT HAS BEEN MY PLEASURE to introduce you to the treasures of Tibetan meditation. As I pointed out in the introduction, Tibetan meditation is a main component of Tibetan Buddhism that traditionally has been only available to Buddhists. As a Lama living in a Western country, my experience has taught me that the practical aspects of Tibetan meditation are also very beneficial to people of different creeds and non-believers. The various methods I have introduced to you in this book are part of the knowledge gained in Buddhist mind training that emerged millennia ago.

I have made it my task to bring to you these jewels from the Tibetan treasures and have augmented them according to my practical experience, so they can be used by all people, on all levels, and with the same benefit, whether they are Buddhist, of another creed, or nonbelievers.

Practical instructions were included to assist you in finding and holding on to inner balance in these hectic modern times. The space and peace you gain through experience will assist you in becoming more relaxed when you deal with the people around you in everyday life. It is not only you who benefits greatly from the practice of the exercises included in this book; there will be positive change in your immediate environment because you are now acting more skillfully, intelligently, and thoughtfully.

There are many of us who make the decision to turn our back on the hectic world to live in peace in a faraway place. Yet no matter where we go, if we have not mastered teaching our mind how to conquer its transgressions, our resentments or negative thoughts will pursue us. As long as the three poisons blind your mind, it will not lose its appetite for worldly desires, and, in looking for satisfaction, will become hostile to any obstacle in its path.

Material things are very important to average people, and it certainly brings joy to our heart when we acquire an item that is beautiful and precious; it is natural and right to be happy about something like that. However, following the golden path is the art in finding your way between secular and spiritual worlds. If we spend all our time chasing after worldly assets, our happiness will not last long, because the nature of worldly riches is that they come and go. If, on the other hand, we spend all our time seeking spiritual wealth, we will find it difficult to survive in a Western society that exaggerates material wealth.

This is precisely where, I believe, practical Tibetan meditation as described in this book can be most effective. When integrated into modern life, the ancient instructions on meditations, combined and augmented by the effective relaxation exercises of the Lü-Gom, are a catalyst for discovering a novel and healthy approach to life. A component of this new and healthy way of life is the appreciation in the art of living your life—in control of your wild mind, instead of at its mercy. This approach to life combines Western and Eastern qualities, and material and spiritual values are seen as equal. A person who has incorporated this healthy philosophy constantly keeps an eye on his or her outer and inner well-being and health and therefore handles any kind of situation well. People like this will acquire a personality of such inner equanimity and strength that it benefits not only themselves but also all the people that are close to them.

Seven jewels I wish you to discover

In the same spirit as the rest of this book, I want to conclude with the seven jewels of Tibetan meditation I wish for you to discover:

- That you will draw true benefit from Tibetan meditation
- That you will experience a noticeably positive change in your life
- That the people around you will sense this positive change and will be inspired
- That endurance and patience will let you reach the happy state of shi nay and recognize the true nature of phenomena
- That the door to inner wisdom will be opened to you in light of that recognition, and that you will therein be connected to your inborn source of love and compassion
- That you will contribute significantly to universal peace and brighten the world as a result of the practice of Tibetan meditation
- That this glow will never wane

—Dagsay Tulku Rinpoche

A Reference Guide to the Exercises

A REFERENCE GUIDE TO THE EXERCISES

NEGATIVE FACTOR	MEDITATIVE REMEDY (Choose One)	PAGE NUMBER
Anger Aggression	Visualization of Breathing	58
	Ninefold Purification of Energy	26
	The Calm State of Mind	103
Hopeless situation	Impermanence of Phenomena	131
	Visualizing the Pure Land	86
	Pooling the Energy of Five Elements	63
	Gentle Phowa Practice	86
Illness	Visualization of Breathing	58
	Collection of Healing Power	53
	Pooling the Energy of Five Elements	63
	Impermanence of Phenomena	131
	Emptiness of Phenomena	126
	Visualizing the Pure Land	86
	Gentle Phowa Practice	86
Aging	Impermanence of Phenomena	131
	Visualizing the Pure Land	86
	Pooling the Energy of Five Elements	63
	Gentle Phowa Practice	86
	Emptiness of Phenomena	126
Process of dying	Impermanence of Phenomena	131
	Visualizing the Pure Land	86
	Emptiness of Phenomena	126
	Love and Compassion	142
	Gentle Phowa Practice	86

EXERCISE (Choose One)	PAGE NUMBER	MANTRA (Choose One)	CD TRACK	POSITIVE EFFECT
Affection	115	Tara mantra	14	Calming down
Tolerance	117	Chenrezi mantra	17	Tolerance
Humility	116	Vijaya Devi mantra	15	
Wisdom	113			
Wisdom	113	Five-elements mantra	8–12	Courage
Negative thoughts	111	Amitabha mantra	16	Acceptance
Tolerance	117	Chenrezi mantra	17	Perseverance
Affection	115			Hope
				Joy of life
Negative thoughts	111	Medicine Buddha mantra	2	Improvement
Wisdom	113	Amitayus mantra	13	Healing
Peace of mind	119	Vijaya Devi mantra	15	Courage
		Tara mantra	14	Acceptance
				Quality of life
				Perseverance
Negative thoughts	111	Chenrezi mantra	17	Equanimity
Wisdom	113	Vajra Guru mantra	19	Optimism
Affection	115	Amitayus mantra	13	Letting go
Humility	116	Tara mantra	14	Perseverance
Peace of mind	119	Vijaya mantra	15	Quality of life
		Amitabha mantra	16	
Peace of mind	119	All mantras		Peaceful and calm process of dying

A REFERENCE GUIDE TO THE EXERCISES

NEGATIVE FACTOR	MEDITATIVE REMEDY (Choose One)	PAGE NUMBER
Stress	Harmonizing Body and Soul	31
	The Calm State of Mind	103
	Collection of Healing Power	53
Depression	Ray-of-light Purification	49
Psychological imbalance	Igniting the Inner Fire	79
Fear and panic	Visualizing the Pure Land	86
Lack of concentration	Ninefold Purification of Energy	26
Forgetfulness	Concentration Meditation	97
Dissatisfaction	Impermanence of Phenomena	131
	Pooling the Energy of Five Elements	63
	Igniting the Inner Fire	79
	The Calm State of Mind	103
Overcoming negative emotions:		
Anger	Ninefold Purification of Energy	26
Arrogance	Color Rain Showers	60
Greed	Nectar Purification	265
Egoism	Igniting the Inner Fire	79
Conceit	Emptiness of Phenomena	126
High-handedness	Patience and Tolerance	137
Pride	Love and Compassion	142
Aggression	Giving and Taking	145
Ignorance	Analytical Meditation	121
Delusion	Analytical Meditation	121
Hatred	Harmonizing Body and Soul, Love and Compassion	31, 142

EXERCISE (Choose One)	PAGE NUMBER	MANTRA (Choose One)	CD TRACK	POSITIVE EFFECT
Modesty	110	Tara mantra	14	Relaxation
Negative thoughts	111	Five-elements mantra	8–12	Equanimity
				Peacefulness
Tolerance	117	Vijaya Devi mantra	15	
Affection	115	Tara mantra	14	Balance
Negative thoughts	111	Medicine Buddha mantra	2	Joyfulness
				Equanimity
Peace of mind	119	Vjara Guru mantra	19	Happiness
				Love of life
Wisdom	113	Manjushri mantra	18	Alertness
Tolerance	117	Tara mantra	14	Mental stability
				Clear mind
Five meditations on pooling the energy of five elements	63	Five-elements mantras	8–12	Moderation
		Chenrezi mantra	17	Happiness
				Contentment
Affection	115	Vajra sattva mantra	1	Friendship
Humility	116	Purification mantras	3–7	Peace
Peace of mind	119	Chenrezi mantra	17	Equanimity
Modesty	111	Vajra Guru mantra	19	Harmony
Negative thoughts	111	Tara mantra	14	Love
		Medicine Buddha mantra	2	Compassion
				Respect
				Good sense

Seminars and Projects

Seminars

If you are interested in seminars on basic Tibetan meditation or advanced courses that follow the teaching of Lama Dagsay Tulku, or if you would like to participate in a workshop on the introduction to practical Tibetan Buddhism, write to the following address:

> Lama Dagsay Tulku
> Postfach
> CH-8833 Samstagern
> Switzerland

Projects

With the support of relatives and friends, Dagsay Tulku Rinpoche has initiated several Tibetan projects: the reconstruction of the Chokri Monastery, the construction of a clinic near the monastery, the manufacture of Tibetan remedies, the cultivation of Tibetan medicinal plants, and the formation of classes to teach Tibetan medicine.

Songs of the Mantras

by Dechen Shak-Dagsay

IN 1999 DECHEN SHAK-DAGSAY, daughter of Lama Dagsay Tulku, created the CD *Dewa Che*, containing original singing of the mantras described throughout this text. Accompanied by wonderful music, *Dewa Che* is the perfect musical compliment to the chanted mantras on the CD included with this book. If you wish to order the musical version of the mantras as performed by Dechen Shak-Dagsay, contact Polyglobe music at www.polyglobemusic.com or send an order request to PB 844, A-6023, Innsbruck, Austria.

Annotated Bibliography

The Fourteenth Dalai Lama. *Kindness, Clarity, and Insight*. Ithaca, N.Y.: Snow Lion, 1984.
A wonderful book explaining the steps to enlightenment in Tibetan Buddhism.

Karta, Lama. *Eine Einführung in die Lehre Buddhas*. Munich: Barth, 1999.
Lama Karta describes the history, nature, and practice of Buddhism.

Rinpoche, Chökyi Nyima. *The Bardo Guidebook*. Kathmandu: Ranjung Yeshe, 1991.
The author explains the teachings of the Bardo in relation to an important classical text. He explains the "states in between," meaning the different stages of life that a human will pass through during his or her lifetime, such as birth, death, and reincarnation. Not recommended for beginners.

Rinpoche, Samdhong. *Buddhistische Meditation*. Sattledorf, Germany: Adyar, 1996.
A series of essays. The author answers questions that anyone who meditates will be interested in, including a great number of helpful hints for beginners.

Rinpoche, Sogyal. *The Tibetan Book of Living and Dying*. San Francisco: HarperSanFrancisco, 1993.
This book addresses not only theoretical questions in regard to death and dying but also offers practical advice in understanding life and death. The language is easy to follow and the content is interesting for the beginner as well as the advanced student.

Thondup, Tulku et al. *Boundless Healing: Meditation Exercises to Enlighten the Mind and Heal the Body.* Boston: Shambhala Publications, 2000.
The clearly formulated and easily applicable exercises in this book will help you in applying Buddhist practice in dealing with everyday problems.

Thurman, Robert, trans. *The Tibetan Book of the Dead.* New York: Bantam Doubleday, 1993.
A rather demanding new translation and newly annotated edition of the *Tibetan Book of the Dead,* which unfolds the full extent of the Tibetan art of dying to the Western reader.

Index

About the Author

DAGSAY TULKU RINPOCHE WAS BORN in Tibet in 1936. He is one of the first Tibetan Lamas to settle in Switzerland.

When he was two years old, Dagsay Tulku was discovered to be the reincarnation of the Fifth Dagsay, one of the main Lamas of the Chokri Monastery in the Eastern Tibetan city of Tehor. He was raised there under the guidance of the monk Rigzin Dorje, a great master of Buddhist teachings. At the young age of only ten years, Lama Dagsay already carried out the religious responsibilities of one of the main Lamas in the monastery, which consisted of about five hundred monks at that time. Following the uprising of the Tibetan people against the Chinese occupation, he fled to India in 1959. Because of fortunate circumstances, he had the opportunity to study Sanskrit and Buddhist philosophy at the University of Benares. In 1963 the Fourteenth Dalai Lama unexpectedly requested Lama Dagsay to act as a spiritual leader for the Tibetan refugees in Switzerland. The country has become a second home to him and his family. He has been working in construction design, always upholding Tibetan spirituality and expanding his knowledge in Tibetan philosophy. He teaches Tibetan meditation for secular application, Buddhist teachings in the steps to enlightenment (Lamrim), and gives blessings and initiations.

The symbol that appears in the beginning of every chapter is Dagsay's personal symbol. The circle stands for the emptiness of phenomena; the flower for compassion; the three spheres the Dharma body, the body of well-being, and the body of reincarnation. The vajra stands for the teachings of the Diamond vehicle.

BOOKS OF RELATED INTEREST

TAMING THE TIGER
Tibetan Teachings on Right Conduct, Mindfulness, and Universal Compassion
by Akong Tulku Rinpoche

ZEN IN MOTION
Lessons from a Master Archer on Breath, Posture, and the Path of Intuition
by Neil Claremon

THE BUDDHIST HANDBOOK
A Complete Guide to Buddhist Schools, Teaching, Practice, and History
by John Snelling

TIBETAN AYURVEDA
Health Secrets from the Roof of the World
by Robert Sachs

THE PASSIONATE BUDDHA
Wisdom on Intimacy and Enduring Love
by Robert Sachs

BUDDHIST MASTERS OF ENCHANTMENT
The Lives and Legends of the Mahasiddhas
Translated by Keith Dowman
Illustrated by Robert Beer

IMMORTALITY AND REINCARNATION
Wisdom from the Forbidden Journey
by Alexandra David-Neel

THE DOCTRINE OF AWAKENING
The Attainment of Self-Mastery According to the Earliest Buddhist Texts
by Julius Evola

Inner Traditions • Bear & Company
P.O. Box 388
Rochester, VT 05767
1-800-246-8648
www.InnerTraditions.com

Or contact your local bookseller